Winter
Knits
made easy

Winter Knits
made easy

DK

DK UK
Senior Designers Jane Ewart and Clare Shedden
Senior Editors Katharine Goddard, Carrie Love, and Nikki Sims
Designers Charlotte Bull and Charlotte Johnson
Editor Anne Hildyard
US Editor Margaret Parrish
US Senior Editor Shannon Beatty
Managing Editor Penny Smith
Managing Art Editor Marianne Markham
Senior Jacket Creative Nicola Powling
Production Editor Raymond Williams
Production Controller Che Creasey
Photography Ruth Jenkinson
Art Direction for Photography Jane Ewart
Art Director Jane Bull
Publisher Mary Ling

DK INDIA
Senior Editor Dorothy Kikon
Editor Aditi Batra
Art Editor Swati Katyal
Managing Editor Alicia Ingty
Managing Art Editor Navidita Thapa
Pre-Production Manager Sunil Sharma
Senior DTP Designer Pushpak Tyagi
DTP Designer Satish Gaur

First American Edition, 2014
Published in the United States by DK Publishing
4th floor, 345 Hudson Street, New York, New York 10014

14 15 16 17 18 10 9 8 7 6 5 4 3 2 1
001—192949—September/2014
Copyright © 2014 Dorling Kindersley Limited
All rights reserved.

A catalog record for this book is available from the Library of Congress.
ISBN 978-1-4654-2466-2

DK books are available at special discounts when purchased in bulk for sales
promotions, premiums, fund-raising, or educational use. For details, contact: DK
Publishing Special Markets, 345 Hudson Street, New York, New York 10014 or
SpecialSales@dk.com.

Printed and bound in China by South China Printing Co. Ltd.

Discover more at
www.dk.com/crafts

Introduction

Leafing through the pages of Winter Knits will elicit many "oohs" and "aahs," since this creative collection showcases gorgeous items for every member of the family (from the supercute baby and toddler items, through the adorable children's projects up to the stylish adult section) as well as many stunning items soon to be treasured in your home.

The patterns in this beautiful and inspirational book are suitable for all knitters—from complete beginners (try the "Easy" projects) to those looking for their next knitting challenge, be that trying out a cable or a colorful motif pattern.

With 40 projects ranging from a child's simple scarf and pom-pom baby hat to a chunky cable blanket and Fair Isle sweater, you'll find there is a pattern for everyone, no matter what your style or level of knitting ability. The most difficult decision will be: what to knit first?

In addition to the myriad projects, there is a section that gives any knitter the need-to-know information on techniques—from the basic knit and purl stitches and some useful ways of casting on and off, to how to shape your knitting and work multicolored Fair Isle and intarsia, plus ideas to help you finish off a project with flair (be it creating buttonholes or making pom-poms). Here you will also find helpful information about different fiber choices and selecting yarns and equipment when planning your knitting. The essential techniques—all shown with step-by-step photographs—can help a beginner or intermediate knitter with the how-to of knitting, but will also give the more experienced knitter inspiration for superb details to add to their pieces for a truly professional end result.

Whichever patterns you choose, happy knitting!

Contents

Babies and toddlers 8

Simple baby beanie hat 10
Baby pom-pom hat 12
Baby Fair Isle cardigan 14
Simple striped sweater 20
Circles crib blanket 26
Baby booties 30
Toddler's socks 32
Baby mittens 36

Children 38

Norwegian sweater 40
Color block sweater 44
Fair Isle sweater dress 48
Child's beanie hat 54
Child's striped scarf 56
Child's cowl hood 60
Child's hat with ear flaps 62
Sheep scarf with pockets 66
Hooded scarf 70
Child's easy mittens 74
Ear warmer headband 76

Women 80

Easy Fair Isle sweater 82
Cable and bobble sweater 86
Partial Fair Isle sweater 90
Cabled bobble hat 96
Slouchy hat 98
Wrist warmers 100
Ruched scarf 104
Short cabled socks 106
Boot cuffs 110

Men 112

Textured sweater 114
Ribbed socks 118
Beanie hat 122
Cabled scarf 124
Slouchy hat 126

Home 128

Chunky cable lap blanket 130
Patchwork blanket 132
Snowflake pillow 138
Fair Isle coasters 142
Cabled pillow cover 144
Toy basket 146
Fair Isle Christmas ornaments 148

Tools and equipment 152

Yarns 154
Other equipment 170

Techniques 172

Key techniques 174
Following stitch patterns 194
Increases and decreases 198
Cables and twists 212
Colorwork 214
Short rows 222
Circular knitting 224
Correcting mistakes 227
Finishing details 228
Embellishments 244

Glossary 248
Index 251
Acknowledgments 256

Projects for
Babies &
Toddlers

top tip

Choosing a variegated
yarn adds extra interest
to an otherwise
plain item.

Simple baby beanie hat

This adorable hat is a great starter project for trying knitting in the round. The pattern is simple and the shaping of the beanie's crown uses an easy decrease, too. And, because stockinette stitch naturally curls at the edges, this hat even creates its own brim.

you will need

DIFFICULTY Easy

SIZE To fit a child age
0-6 (6-12:12-18) months

YARN
Plymouth Dreambaby DK 50g

A x 2

NEEDLES
4 x US6 (4mm/UK8)
double-pointed needles

GAUGE
22sts x 30 rows over 4in
(10cm) in st st

NOTIONS
Darning needle

How to make

Cast on 64 (80:96) sts plus 1 extra st and share between three needles. To "join in the round," slip the extra stitch onto the left needle and then knit first and last stitches together before following the pattern (see also p.224). K every round until work measures 5½ (6¼:7)in (14 (16:18)cm).

Shape crown
ROUND 1: *K6, k2tog, rep from * to end of round. (56 (70:84) sts)
ROUND 2: K.
ROUND 3: *K5, k2tog, rep from * to end of round. (48 (60:72) sts)
ROUND 4: K.
ROUND 5: *K4, k2tog, rep from * to end of round. (40 (50:60) sts)
ROUND 6: K.
ROUND 7: *K3, k2tog, rep from * to end of round. (32 (40:48) sts)
ROUND 8: K.
ROUND 9: *K2, k2tog, rep from * to end of round. (24 (30:36) sts)
ROUND 10: K.
ROUND 11: *K1, k2tog, rep from * to end of round. (16 (20:24) sts)
ROUND 12: K.

ROW 13: * K2tog, rep from * to end of round. (8 (10:12) sts)
ROW 14: K.
Break yarn, thread through remaining stitches, pull tightly, and weave through to WS.

Finishing
Sew in all ends with a darning needle and block (see p.238).

◄ This beanie hat uses
Plymouth Yarn Company
Dreambaby DK Prints #210.

top tip
Multicolored pom-poms are a great way of using up scraps of leftover yarn.

Baby pom-pom hat

Pep up a simple knitted piece with a cable pattern to make this cute baby hat. Don't be scared of cabling—it's easy to do and the results are impressive. Here, the cuteness is maximized with the addition of two pom-poms that coordinate with the rib of the brim.

you will need

DIFFICULTY Easy

SIZE To fit 0–6-month-old baby

YARN
Sublime Extra Fine Merino Wool DK 50g

A x 1   B x 1

NEEDLES
1 pair of US6 (4mm/UK8) needles
Cable needle

GAUGE
20sts x 27 rows over 4in (10cm) in st st

NOTIONS
Darning needle

SPECIAL ABBREVIATIONS
C3B Place 3 sts on cable needle (cn) and hold at back of work, k3, k3 from cn.
C3F Place 3 sts on cn and hold at front of work, k3, k3 from cn.

How to make

Brim
Using yarn B, cast on 84sts.
ROW 1: K1 [p2, k2] x 20, p2, k1.
ROW 2: P1 [k2, p2] x 20, k2, p1.
ROWS 3–8: Rep rows 1–2.

Crown
Change to yarn A.
ROW 9: K.
ROW 10: P.
ROW 11: K36, C3B, C3F, k36.
ROW 12: P.
ROW 13: K.
ROW 14: P.
ROWS 15–38: Rep rows 9–14.
ROW 39: K.
Cast off knitwise.

Finishing
With WS facing, sew the sides together with a darning needle. Then line up top of seam with center of cable (so you have a central back seam) and sew across the top. Make 2 pom-poms (see p.244) in yarn B and sew on each corner.

◀ This hat is knitted in Sublime Extra Fine Merino Wool DK A: 361 Gem and B: 363 Indigo.

Baby Fair Isle cardigan

Keep your little one toasty and warm but free to roam in this beautiful cardigan. This knit uses two colors along a row and so is a true Fair Isle project—it's just that one ball is a self-striping yarn, which gives the impression of something much more complicated.

❄ you will need

DIFFICULTY Moderate

SIZE To fit a baby age 0–6 (6–12:12–18) months

YARN
Patons Classic Wool DK Superwash and Twisted Fiber Arts Yummy Striping 100g

A x 2   **B** x 1

NEEDLES
A: 1 pair of US6 (4mm/UK8) needles
B: US6 (4mm/UK8) circular needle

GAUGE
22sts and 30 rows over 4in (10cm) in st st

NOTIONS
Darning needle
4 buttons

How to make

Back
Using needles A and yarn B, cast on 58 (64:72) sts.
K 4 rows.
Join in yarn A.
Cont in st st and foll the chart starting at st 1 and ending at st 58 (4:12), from row 1 to row 40 (46:60).
Cont in yarn A only.
K 2 rows.

Shape armholes
Dec 1 st at each end of next 7 rows. (44 (50:58) sts)
Cont without further shaping until armhole measures 5(5¼:5½)in (12(13:14)cm), ending on a WS row.

Shape shoulders
Cast off 7 (8:9) sts at beg of next 2 rows. (30 (34:40) sts)
Cast off 8 (9:10) sts at beg of next 2 rows. (14 (16:20) sts)
Cast off rem 14 (16:20) sts.

Left front
Using needles A and yarn B, cast on 27 (30:34) sts.
K 4 rows.
Join in yarn A. ***
Cont in st st and foll the chart starting at st 5 (5:1) and ending at st 31 (34:34), from row 1 to row 40 (46:60).
Cont in yarn A only.
K 2 rows.

Shape armholes
Dec 1 st at armhole edge on next 7 rows. (20 (23:27) sts)
Cont without shaping until armhole measures 3(3½:3½)in (8(9:9)cm), ending with a RS row.

➤ This cardigan uses Patons Classic Wool DK Superwash in A: Aran and Twisted Fiber Arts Yummy Striping in B: Minstrel.

top tip

Having buttons just at the
top of the cardigan allows
its wearer full freedom
of movement.

Shape neck

Cast off 2 (2:3) sts, purl to end of row.
(18 (21:24) sts)
Dec 1 st at neck edge on next 3 (4:5)
rows. (15 (17:19) sts)
Cont without further shaping until
armhole measures 5(5¼:5½)in
(12(13:14)cm), ending with a WS row.

Shape shoulder

Cast off 7 (8:9) sts at the beg of the
next row, k to end of row. (8 (9:10) sts)
NEXT ROW: P.
Cast off rem 8 (9:10) sts.

Right front

Work as for left front to ***.
Cont in st st and foll the chart starting
at st 4 (1:3) and ending at st 30
(30:36), from row 1 to row 40 (46:60).
Cont in yarn A only.
K 2 rows.

Shape armholes

Dec 1 st at armhole edge on next
7 rows 20 (23:27) sts.
Cont without shaping until armhole
measures 3(3½:3½)in (8(9:9)cm),
ending with a WS row.

Shape neck

Cast off 2 (2:3) sts, k to end of row.
(18 (21:24) sts)
Dec 1 st at neck edge on next
3 (4:5) rows. (15 (17:19) sts)
Cont without further shaping until
armhole measures 5(5¼:5½)in
(12(13:14)cm), ending with a RS row.

Shape shoulder

Cast off 7 (8:9) sts at the beg of
the next row, purl to end of row.
(8 (9:10) sts)
NEXT ROW: K.
Cast off rem 8 (9:10) sts.

Sleeves

Using needles A and yarn B,
cast on 34 (36:36) sts.
K 4 rows.
Join in yarn A.

Cont in st st and foll the chart starting
at st 1 (6:6) and ending at st 34
(41:41), from row 1 to row 57 (64:75),
and inc 1 st at each end on 5th and
every foll 4th row, working extra sts
into Fair Isle patt.

Neckband and front band

Join shoulder seams. Using yarn B and
needle B, and with RS facing, pick up
(see p.228) and k57 (66:79) sts up
right front and right neck shaping,
12 (14:18) sts across back neck, 57
(66:79) sts down left neck shaping
and left front. (126 (146:176) sts)
K 1 row.

Buttonholes

K32 (38:48) sts, * yo, k2tog, k3, rep
from * three times, k to end of row.
K 3 rows. Cast off.

Finishing

Darn in all yarn ends and block (see
p.238). Sew in the sleeves, placing
center of sleeve to shoulder seam.
Sew side and sleeve seams. Finish by
sewing buttons onto the front band.

Focus on Fair Isle Looking at the detail
of the motif used here, along with the
color-changing yarn, you can see how
impressive the finished pattern appears.

Chart

Key

☐ A: Aran
■ B: Minstrel

Simple striped sweater

Because this project uses stockinette stitch, you get a soft roll at the sleeves, hem, and neckline. The bands of color here are created in a self-striping tweed yarn, so don't worry that the stripes on the arms don't exactly match the stripes of the body.

❄ you will need

DIFFICULTY Easy

SIZE To fit a child age 1-2 (2-3:3-4) years

YARN
Regia Highland Tweed 100g and Patons Classic Wool DK Superwash 50g

A x 1   **B** x 3 (3:4)

NEEDLES
A: 1 pair of US6 (4mm/UK8) needles
B: A US6 (4mm/UK8) circular needle

GAUGE
20sts and 26 rows over 4in (10cm) in st st

NOTIONS
2 stitch holders
Darning needle

How to make

Back
Using needles A and yarn A, cast on 68 (74:80) sts.
Work 6 rows in st st.
Change to yarn B.
Cont in st st and work 20 rows.
Join in yarn A.
Cont in st st in the foll stripe sequence:
ROWS 1–2: 2 rows in yarn A.
ROWS 3–4: 2 rows in yarn B.
Rep rows 1–4, four times more.
Cont in st st with yarn B, until work measures 15(17:19)in (38(43:48)cm) from cast on, ending with a WS row.

Shape shoulders
Cast off 10 (11:12) sts at beg of next 4 rows. Leave rem 28 (30:32) sts on a stitch holder.

◄This sweater is knitted in Regia Highland Tweed 2761 Chestnut (A) and Patons Classic Wool DK Superwash 2012 Cork (B).

Front

Work as for back until front measures 13½(15:16½)in (34(38:42)cm), ending with a WS row.

Shape neck

(Work each side separately.)
K26 (28:30) sts and leave rem sts on a holder.
Dec 1 st at neck edge on every row until you have 20 (22:24) sts rem.
Work the decreases as foll:
On WS rows, p2, p2tog, p to end.
On RS rows, k to last 4sts, k2tog, k2.
Cont until front measures 15(17:19)in (38(43:48)cm) ending with a WS row.

Shape shoulders

Cast off 10 (11:12) sts at beg of next row.
P.
Cast off rem 10 (11:12) sts.
Place center 16 (18:20) sts on a stitch holder.
Rejoin yarn to rem sts and complete second side to match.
Work the decreases as foll:
On RS rows, k2, k2tog tbl, k to end.
On WS rows, p to last 4sts, p2tog tbl, p2.

Sleeves

Using needles A and yarn A, cast on 34 (36:38) sts.

Work in st st and stripe sequence as for back.
At the same time, inc 1 st (by knitting into the front and back of the st) at each end of 7th row and every foll 6th row until there are 54 (58:62) sts.
Cont until sleeve measures 10(11:12¼)in (25(28:31)cm).
Cast off.

Neckband

Join right shoulder seam.
Using yarn B and needle B, pick up and k10 (12:14) sts down left front neck.
K16 (18:20) sts from center front holder, pick up and k10 (12:14) sts up right front neck, k28 (30:32) sts from back neck holder. (64 (72:80) sts)
P.
Change to yarn A and work 8 rows in st st.
Cast off very loosely.

Finishing

Join left shoulder seam. Sew in sleeves, placing center of sleeve to shoulder seam. Join side and shoulder seams.

Colors of a similar hue
The tones of the stripes of this sweater change subtly across the piece but work as bright accents overall.

top tip

Be sure to match the stripes on the front and the back when sewing the seams.

Circles crib blanket

Supersoft and perfect for snuggling, this multicolored blanket is a great pattern for those wanting to try out the intarsia method of colorwork (see p.220). The striking one-color garter-stitch border brings the whole blanket together.

❋ you will need

DIFFICULTY Moderate

SIZE 24½ x 34¼in (62 x 87cm)

YARN
Debbie Bliss Cashmerino
Aran 50g

A x 3   **B** x 2   **C** x 3   **D** x 1

NEEDLES
1 pair of US8
(5mm/UK6) needles

GAUGE
19sts and 25 rows over
4in (10cm) in st st

NOTIONS
Darning needle

How to make

With yarn C, cast on 119sts.
Work 9 rows in g st.
ROW 1: K7 in C, k105 in A, k7 in C.
ROW 2: K7 in C, p105 in A, k7 in C.
ROWS 3–18: Rep these 2 rows
8 times more.
ROW 19: K7 in C, using the intarsia method, k across 35sts row 1 (chart 1), 35sts row 1 (chart 2), 35sts row 1 (chart 1), k7 in C.
ROW 20: K7 in C, p across 35sts row 2 (chart 1), 35sts row 2 (chart 2), 35sts row 2 (chart 1), k7 in C.
ROWS 21–64: These 2 rows set the patt. Cont to follow the charts until the 46 rows are completed.
ROWS 65–82: As rows 1–18.
ROW 83: K7 in C, k 35sts row 1 (chart 2), 35sts row 1 (chart 1), 35sts row 1 (chart 2), k7 in C.
ROW 84: K7 in C, p 35sts row 2 (chart 2), 35sts row 2 (chart 1), 35sts row 2 (chart 2), k7 in C.
ROWS 85–128: Follow the charts as set until 46 rows have been completed.
ROWS 129–146: As rows 1–18.

ROWS 147–210: As rows 19–82.
With yarn C only, work 9 rows in g st.
Cast off knitwise.

Finishing

Weave in all ends with a darning needle and block (see p.238).

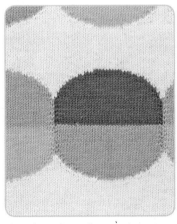

Changing colors When you change color mid-row, wrap the yarns by bringing the next one under the last.

◀ This crib blanket uses Debbie Bliss Cashmerino Aran in A: Ecru, B: Silver, C: Cowslip, and D: Lime.

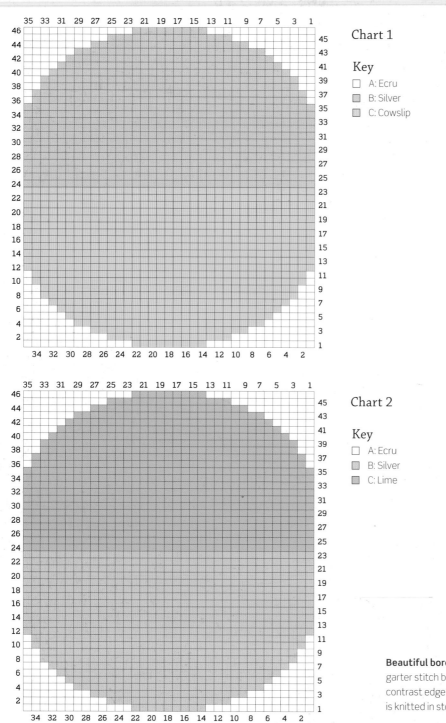

Chart 1

Key

☐ A: Ecru
▨ B: Silver
▨ C: Cowslip

Chart 2

Key

☐ A: Ecru
▨ B: Silver
▨ C: Lime

Beautiful borders The yellow garter stitch border creates a fabulous contrast edge to the blanket, which is knitted in stockinette stitch.

Baby booties

Knitting a baby project is a great way to learn new techniques because the pieces themselves are small. These cute little booties in garter stitch use two yarn colors and a yarn-over increase (see p.203) to create the stripes and shaping in a supersoft cotton.

❄ you will need

DIFFICULTY Easy

SIZE To fit a newborn baby

YARN
Rowan Softknit Cotton 50g

A x 1   **B** x 1

NEEDLES
1 pair of US6 (4mm/UK8) needles

GAUGE
20sts and 28 rows over 4in (10cm) in st st

NOTIONS
Darning needle

How to make

Booties (make 2)

Sole
In yarn A, cast on 27sts.
ROW 1: K.
ROW 2: K1, yo, k12, yo, k1, yo, k12, yo, k1. (31sts)
ROW 3: K.
ROW 4: K1, yo, k14, yo, k1, yo, k14, yo, k1. (35sts)
ROW 5: K.
ROW 6: K1, yo, k16, yo, k1, yo, k16, yo, k1. (39sts)
ROWS 7–17: Change to yarn B and cont in g st.

Shape toe
ROW 18: K15, k2tog, k5, s1, k1, psso, s1, yo, turn.
ROW 19: Using yarn A, k2tog, k5, s1, k1, psso, yo, s1, turn.
ROW 20: Using yarn A, k2tog, k5, s1, k1, psso, s1, yo, turn.
ROW 21: Using yarn B, k2tog, k5, s1, k1, psso, yo, s1, turn.

ROW 22: Using yarn B, k2tog, k5, s1, k1, psso, s1, yo, turn.
ROW 23: Using yarn A, k2tog, k5, k2tog, yo, s1, turn.
ROW 24: Using yarn A, k2tog, k5, s1, k1, psso, s1, yo, turn.
ROW 25: Using yarn B, k2tog, k5, k2tog, yo, s1, turn.
ROW 26: Using yarn B, k2tog, k5, s1, k1, psso, k to end of row. (21sts)
ROW 27: Using yarn A, k.
ROW 28: Using yarn A, k.
ROW 29: Change to yarn B and cont in g st changing color every 4 rows until you have knitted 4in (10cm).

Finishing
Sew in all the loose ends. Using mattress stitch (see p.239), sew up from the sole until you get 2in (5cm) from the top, reverse and sew on the reverse side so that when the top of the bootie is rolled over you will not see the stitching.

◄ These booties use Rowan Softknit Cotton in A: 580 Marina and B: 570 Cream.

top tip
Sewing the seam with
mattress stitch (see p.239)
makes a more comfy
seam for little feet.

Toddler's socks

Small versions of socks can be knitted quickly and spur you on to knit more. These colorful socks have ribbed sections on the tops, heels, and toes to make them strong and durable while keeping them comfy and easy to put on—essential for those with little hands.

❄ you will need

DIFFICULTY Moderate

SIZE To fit a baby/toddler age 3-9 (12-18:24-36) months

YARN
Debbie Bliss Baby Cashmerino 50g

A x 1 **B** x 1 **C** x 1

NEEDLES
1 pair of US3 (3.25mm/UK10) needles
Spare needle

GAUGE
25sts and 34 rows over 4in (10cm) in st st

NOTIONS
Stitch holder
Darning needle

How to make

Socks (make 2)
Using yarn A, cast on 38 (42:46) sts.
Work 4 rows of k1, p1 rib.
Working in st st, work stripe sequence as follows:
ROWS 1-2: Yarn A.
ROWS 3-6: Yarn B.
ROWS 7-8: Yarn C.
Rep these 8 rows once, then rep rows 1-4 (1-8, 1-8) once, then FOR 3RD SIZE ONLY rep rows 1-6, dec 1 st at center of last row on all sizes. (37 (41:45) sts)
Break off yarns.

Divide for heel
Slip first 9 (10:11) sts onto needle, slip next 19 (21:23) sts onto st holder, slip rem 9 (10:11) sts onto spare needle.
With WS facing, join yarn C to instep edge of first 9 (10:11) sts and p to end, cont the row and p across the last 9 (10:11) sts. (18 (20:22) sts)
NEXT ROW: K1, *k1, s1 purlwise; rep from * to last st, k1.
NEXT ROW: P.
Rep the last 2 rows 3 (4:5) times.

Turn heel
ROW 1: K9 (11:13) sts, skpo, k1, turn.
ROW 2: P2 (4:6), p2tog, p1, turn.
ROW 3: K3 (5:7) sts, skpo, k1, turn.
ROW 4: P4 (6:8) sts, p2tog, p1, turn.
ROW 5: K5 (7:9) sts, skpo, k1, turn.
ROW 6: P6 (8:10) sts, p2tog, p1, turn.
ROW 7: K7 (9:11) sts, skpo, k1, turn.
ROW 8: P8 (10:12) sts, p2tog, p1.
(10 (12:14) sts)
Break off yarn.

◄ These socks are knitted in Debbie Bliss Baby Cashmerino in A: Baby Blue, B: Apple, and C: Teal.

Join in yarn B (A:C) with RS facing. Pick up and k6 (7:8) sts along side edge of heel, k5 (6:7) sts, M1, k5 (6:7) sts, pick up and k6 (7:8) sts along other side of heel. (23 (27:31) sts)
P 1 row.

ROWS 1–2: Keeping continuity of stripes, k 1 row, p 1 row.

ROW 3: K1, skpo, k to last 3sts, k2tog, k1.

ROW 4: P.

Rep these 4 rows 1 (2:3) times more. (19 (21:23) sts)
Work another 13 (15:17) rows. Length of foot can be adjusted at this point.

Shape toe

*Using yarn B only:

ROW 1: K1, skpo, (k1, p1), rep to last 4sts, k1, k2tog, k1. (17 (19:21) sts)

ROW 2: K1, p2tog (k1, p1), rep to last 4sts, k1, p2tog tbl, k1.
(15 (17:19) sts)
Rep these 2 rows once more.
(11 (13:15) sts)*
Leave these sts on a holder.

NEXT ROW: Join in yarn B (A:C), with RS facing, k across 19 (21:23) sts left on holder for upper foot.
Cont in stripes as set until 22 (28:34) rows have been worked.
Work toe shaping from * to * as for sole, leave sts on holder.
With RS facing each other, p tog 1st from each needle and cast off as each st is worked.

Finishing

Join the back and side seams using mattress stitch and a large-eyed needle (see pp.239–241).

◄ These socks are knitted in Debbie Bliss Baby Cashmerino in A: Candy Pink, B: Apple, and C: Silver.

top tip
To keep little fingers from
catching on inside seams,
use mattress stitch or
a neat whipstitch.

Baby mittens

Keep little fingernails out of harm's way inside these wonderfully soft and snug mittens. When you're taking Baby out and about, keep tiny hands warm and toasty without risking losing a mitten by knitting an I-cord (see p.75) to join mittens together.

you will need

DIFFICULTY Easy

SIZE To fit a baby age 0–3 months

YARN
Cascade Ultra Pima DK 50g

A x 1

NEEDLES
A: 1 pair of US3 (3.25mm/UK10) needles
B: 1 pair of US6 (4mm/UK8) needles

GAUGE
23sts and 32 rows over 4in (10cm) in st st on US6 (4mm/UK8) needles

NOTIONS
Darning needle

◄ These mittens are made in Cascade Yarns Utra Pima in 3711 China Pink.

How to make

Mittens (make 2)
Using needles A, cast on 29sts.
ROW 1: [K1, p1] x 14, k1.
ROW 2: [P1, k1] x 14, p1.
ROWS 3–7: Rep rows 1–2 twice, then row 1 once.
Change to needles B.
ROW 8: P9, [yo, p2tog, p2] x 3, p8.
ROW 9: K9, [yo, k2tog, k2] x 3, k8.
ROWS 10–24: Rep rows 8–9 seven times, then row 8 once.
ROW 25: K6, s1, k2tog, psso, k4, yo, k2tog, k5, s1, k2tog, psso, k6. (25sts)
ROW 26: P5, s1, p2tog, psso, p3, yo, p2tog, p4, s1, p2tog, psso, p5. (21sts)
ROW 27: K4, s1, k2tog, psso, k2, yo, k2tog, k3, s1, k2tog, psso, k4. (17sts)
ROW 28: P3, s1, p2tog, psso, p5, s1, p2tog, psso, p3. (13sts)
ROW 29: K2, s1, k2tog, psso, k3, s1, k2tog, psso, k2. (9sts)
Cast off tightly knitwise.

Finishing
With right sides facing, join shaped edges and use a neat mattress stitch (see p.239) to close the top and back seams. Mattress stitch makes an ideal, smooth seam for small items. For very little babies, you may want to add elastic around the wrists, which you can always take out later as the baby grows bigger.

Look, no thumbs! Prevent a newborn baby from scratching him/herself with these thumbless mittens that are oh-so soft.

Projects for
Children

Norwegian sweater

The motifs sing loud in this two-color patterned unisex sweater that uses the Fair Isle technique. The beautiful two-colored rib at the cuffs, hem, and neck continues the story of blue and cream. And the wide, buttoned neck makes it easy to put on.

❄ you will need

DIFFICULTY Moderate

SIZE To fit a child age
2-3 (4-5:6-8) years

Actual measurements:
Chest   24½ (27½:30¾)in
        (62 (70:78)cm)

YARN
Patons Classic Wool DK
Superwash DK 50g

A x 4 (5:6)   **B** x 3 (3:4)

NEEDLES
1 pair of US6
(4mm/UK8) needles

GAUGE
24sts and 25 rows to 4in
(10cm) worked over patt

NOTIONS
Stitch holder
Darning needle
6 x ½in (15mm) buttons

NOTE
Weave in the floating yarn
when it passes 3 or more sts,
being careful not to pull it.

How to make

Back

Make a slipknot on needle using both yarns A and B, slip B off the needle so the first st on the needle is A, *cast on 1 st using B, cast on 1 st using A; rep from * until you have cast on 75 (83:93) sts.
Work in striped rib as foll:
ROW 1 (RS): P1A, yb, *k1B, bring yarn A forward, p1, yb; rep from * to end.
ROW 2: Yarn B forward, K1A, bring yarn A forward, *p1B, yarn A back, k1A, yarn A forward; rep from * to end.
Rep rows 1 and 2 until you have worked 10 rows ending on a WS row. Working in st st throughout, with borders as indicated at each edge and main pattern repeated across row between borders, work 40 rows in pattern from chart A, B, C, then D. Read all odd number (RS) rows from right to left and all even number (WS) rows from left to right, stranding yarn not in use loosely across WS of work,

weaving in when worked over 3 or more sts. The 40 rows form patt. Rep chart A, then 4 (6:10) rows of chart B, ending on a WS row.

Shape armhole

Keeping chart patt correct throughout, cast off 4sts at beg of next 2 rows. (67 (75:85) sts).
Dec 1 st at each end of next 3 rows. (61 (69:79) sts).
Cont working in patt without shaping until you have worked another 18 (26:36) rows.
Work in striped rib for 4 rows.

Shoulders

Rib 15 (17:19) sts, cast off center 31 (35:41) sts loosely in rib as set, rib to end of row.
Work 4 rib rows on rem 15 (17:19) sts, then cast off.
Rejoin yarn to right shoulder, rib 4 rows, then cast off.

> This sweater uses Patons Classic Wool DK Superwash in A: Aran and B: Royal Blue.

top tip

Use any of the motifs
on its own to enliven
a plain sweater.

Front

Work as for the back, working all armhole shaping and continuing until you have worked 14 (22:32) rows without shaping.

Shape front neck

Cont in chart patt throughout.

K18 (20:22) sts, turn.

Dec 1 st at neck edge on next 3 rows. (15 (17:19) sts)

Break yarn and leave sts on a holder. With RS facing, transfer rem 43 (49:57) sts to RH needle.

With WS facing, rejoin yarn and p 18 (20:22) sts, turn.

Dec 1 st at neck edge on next 3 rows. (15 (17:19) sts).

With RS facing and working in striped rib, work across 15 (17:19) sts from left shoulder, pick up and k3 down the front neck, then work across 25 (29:35) sts from front neck, pick up and k3 up neck edge, then work across 15 (17:19) sts from right shoulder. (61 (69:79) sts).

Work 1 row.

NEXT ROW (BUTTONHOLE): Rib 2 (3:4), [cast off 2, rib2 (3sts on needle)] x 2, cast off 2, rib until you have 33 (39:47) sts on needle after last buttonhole, [cast off 2, rib2 (3sts on needle)] x 2,

cast off 2, rib to end.

NEXT ROW: Work rib, cast on 2sts over buttonholes to end of row.

Cast off.

Sleeves (make 2)

Cast on as for the back until you have 35 (39:43) sts.

Work in striped rib for 10 rows, ending on a WS row.

ROW 1 (RS): Using yarn A, k into front and back of first stitch, k2 (3:4) sts, m1, k2 (3:4) sts, m1, *k3 (3:4) sts, m1; rep from * to last 3 (2:2) sts. Finish this row as foll:

For 1st size only

M1, k2, k into front and back of last st. (49sts)

For 2nd & 3rd sizes only

K1, k into front and back of last st. (53:55) sts)

ROW 2: P.

Cont work in st st. Set up patt as foll:

ROW 3 (RS): K2 (4:1)A, rep sleeve chart A row 3 across row to last 2 (4:0) sts, k2 (4:0)A.

Cont working from 4th to 12th row of chart A (WS), with borders as set, then rows 1–4 of chart B, then rep 6 rows of chart C.

At the same time, inc 1 st at both ends of the 5th and every foll 4th

row until there are 73 (67:75) sts, working the new sts into the patt.

For 2nd and 3rd sizes only

Cont to inc 1 st at each end of every foll 6th row until there are (77:83) sts.

All sizes

Cont to rep 6 rows of chart C until sleeve measures 11 (12¼:13½)in (28 (31:34)cm) from beg, ending on a WS row.

Shape sleeve head

Cont with chart C, cast off 4sts at beg of next 2 rows. (65 (69:75) sts)

Then dec 1 st at each end of the next 5 rows. (55 (59:65) sts)

Cast off.

Finishing

Block (see p.238) according to the ballband. Overlap the back shoulder ribs so that the front band with buttonholes covers the extended shoulder. Catch stitch the sleeve edge together. Join side and sleeve seams, being careful to match the patterns. Sew in sleeves matching the center of the sleeve to the shoulder. Sew buttons onto the back extended shoulder so they correspond with the front buttonholes.

Chart A

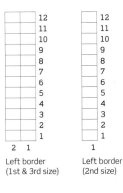

Left border
(1st & 3rd size)

Left border
(2nd size)

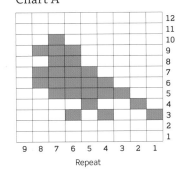

Repeat

Chart A—sleeve

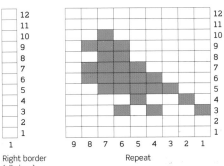

Right border
(all sizes)

Repeat

Chart B

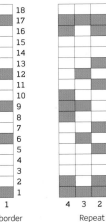

Left border
(2nd & 3rd size) 1st
size has no left border

Repeat

Right border
(all sizes)

Chart B—sleeve

Repeat

Chart C

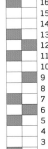

Left border
(1st & 3rd size)

Left border
(2nd size)

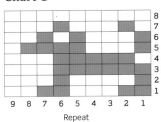

Repeat

Right border
(all sizes)

Chart C—sleeve

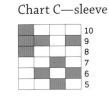

Chart D

Left border
(2nd & 3rd size) 1st
size has no left border

Repeat

Right border
(all sizes)

Key

☐ A: Aran
◼ B: Royal Blue

Color block sweater

This striking sweater uses bold ribs and color blocking to great effect. The wide rib and yoke in the accent color provide detail, while the same rib in the main color provides sturdy cuffs and a fitted hem. Knit a wardrobe of these sweaters in various color combinations.

you will need

DIFFICULTY Easy

SIZE To fit a child age
2–3 (4-5:6-7:8-9) years
Actual measurements:
Chest   27½(29½:31½:33½)in
(70(75:80:85)cm)

Length to shoulder
14(16½:19:21)in
(36(42:48:54)cm)

Sleeve   9½(11½:13½:15)in
(24(29:34:38)cm)

YARN
Debbie Bliss Rialto Aran 50g

A x 4 (5:5:6)   **B** x 1 (2:2:2)

NEEDLES
A: 1 pair of US7
(4.5mm/UK7) needles
B: 1 pair of US8 (5mm/UK6)
needles
C: Spare needle

GAUGE
18sts and 24 rows over 4in
(10cm) in st st using US8
(5mm/UK6) needles

NOTIONS
Stitch holder
Darning needle

‹ This sweater is knitted in Debbie
Bliss Rialto Aran A: 001 Stone
and B: 101 Lime.

How to make

Back
Using needles A and yarn A, cast on
62 (66:74:78) sts.
ROW 1: K2, [p2, k2] to end.
ROW 2: P2, [k2, p2] to end.
Rep the last 2 rib rows 5 (6:7:8) times
more, inc 3 (3:1:1) sts evenly across
last row. (65 (69:75:79) sts)
Change to needles B and beg with a k
row, work in st st until back measures
(9(10¾:12½:14½)in) 22(27:32:37)cm
from cast-on edge, ending with
a p row.

Shape armholes
Cast off 5 (6:7:8) sts at beg of next
2 rows. (55 (57:61:63) sts)
Change to yarn B and cont in st st
until back measures 14(16½:19:21)in
(36(42:48:54)cm) from cast-on edge,
ending with a p row.

Shape shoulders
Cast off 7sts at beg of next 2 rows
and 7 (7:8:8) sts at beg of foll 2 rows.
Leave rem 27 (29:31:33) sts on
a holder.

Front
Work as given for back until front
measures 12(14¼:16½:18½)in
(31(36:42:47)cm) from
cast-on edge, ending with a p row.

Shape left neck
NEXT ROW: K18 (18:19:19) sts, turn
and work on these sts only for first
side of front neck. Leave rem sts
on a spare needle.
NEXT ROW: P to end.
NEXT ROW: K to last 3sts, k2tog, k1.
Rep the last 2 rows three more times.
(14 (14:15:15) sts)

Work until front measures
the same as back to shoulder,
ending at armhole edge.

Shape left shoulder
Cast off 7sts at beg of next row.
Work 1 row.
Cast off rem 7 (7:8:8) sts.

Shape right neck
With RS facing, slip center 19
(21:23:25) sts onto a holder, rejoin
yarn to rem sts, k to end.
NEXT ROW: P to end.
NEXT ROW: K1, skpo, k to end.
Rep the last 2 rows three times more.
(14 (14:15:15) sts)
Work until front measures the
same as back to shoulder, ending
at armhole edge.

Shape right shoulder
Cast off 7sts at beg of next row.
Work 1 row.
Cast off rem 7 (7:8:8) sts.

Sleeves (make 2)
Using needles A and yarn A cast on
34 (38:38:42) sts.
ROW 1: K2, [p2, k2] to end.
ROW 2: P2, [k2, p2] to end.

Rep the last 2 rib rows 5 times more
increasing 2 (0:2:0) sts evenly across
the last row. (36 (38:40:42) sts)
Change to needles B and beg with
a k row cont in st st.
Work 4 rows.
INC ROW: K3, M1, k to last 3sts, M1, k3.
Work 5 rows.
Rep the last 6 rows 5 (6:8:9) times
more and the inc row again.
(50 (54:60:64) sts)
Cont straight until sleeve measures
9½(11½:13½:15)in (24(29:34:38)cm)
from cast-on edge, ending with
a p row.
Mark each end of last row with a
colored thread.
Work 6 (6:8:8) rows.
Cast off.

Neckband
Join right shoulder seam.
With RS facing, using needles A and
yarn B, pick up and k14 (16:16:18) sts
down LS of front neck, k across 19
(21:23:25) sts from front neck, pick up
and k14 (16:16:18) sts up RS of front
neck, k across 27 (29:31:33) sts from
back neck. (74 (82:86:94) sts)
ROW 1: K2, [p2, k2] to end.
ROW 2: P2, [k2, p2] to end.

Rep these 2 rows twice more and
the first row again.
Cast off in rib.

Finishing
Join left shoulder and neckband
seam. Matching center of cast-off
edge of sleeve to shoulder, sew on
sleeves, sewing rows above markers
to sts cast off at under arm. Join side
and sleeve seams.

top tip

Use primary colors for boldness, pastels for delicacy, or toning colors for subtle shading.

top tip

To save little fingers from catching in the Fair Isle "floats," weave these in loosely as you work.

Fair Isle sweater dress

This pretty sweater dress has a striking Fair Isle pattern and matching border designs on the cuffs and hem. To transform this into a sweater, suitable for a girl or a boy, just shorten the plain stockinette stitch sections of the back and front to match your measurements.

✳ you will need

DIFFICULTY Moderate

SIZE To fit a child age
4-5 (6-7:8-9:10-11) years
Actual measurements:
Chest   29(30:31:32)in
           (74(77:79:81)cm)
Length to shoulder
           19(21¼:23½:26)in
           (48(54:60:66)cm)
Sleeve 9½(11½:13½:15)in
           (24(29:34:38)cm)

YARN
Rico Merino Aran 50g

A x 5 (5:6:6)   **B** x 1

C x1   **D** x 1

NEEDLES
A: 1 pair of US7
(4.5mm/UK7) needles
B: 1 pair of US8
(5mm/UK6) needles
C: Spare needle

GAUGE
18sts and 24 rows over 4in
(10cm) in st st using US8
(5mm/UK6) needles

NOTIONS
Stitch holder
Darning needle

How to make

Back
Using needles A and yarn B, cast on 66 (70:78:82) sts.
ROW 1: K2, [p2, k2] to end.
Cut off B. Join on yarn A.
ROW 2: P to end.
These 2 rows form the rib.
Rep the last 2 rows 4 times more using yarn A only, inc 3 (3:1:1) sts evenly across last row.
(69 (73:79:83) sts)
Change to needles B and beg with a k row, work 4 rows in st st.
Work from chart 1 as foll:
ROW 1: K1 (3:2:4) in yarn A, work last 2sts of 1st row of patt rep, [work across 1st row of 8st patt rep] 8 (8:9:9) times, work st 1 of 1st row of patt rep, k1 (3:2:4) A.
ROW 2: P1 (3:2:4) A, work st 1 of 2nd row of patt rep, [work across 2nd row of 8st patt rep] 8 (8:9:9) times, work last 2 sts of 2nd row of patt rep, p1 (3:2:4) A.
These 2 rows set chart 1.
Cont in patt to end of chart 1.
Cont in A.
NEXT ROW: P to end, dec 2sts across row. (67 (71:77:81) sts)
Cont in st st until back measures 10½(13:15½:17½)in (27(33:39:44)cm) from cast-on edge, ending with a

WS row.
Work from chart 2 as foll:
ROW 1: Using yarn A, k to end.
ROW 2: Using yarn B, p to end.
ROW 3: Using A, k to end.
ROW 4: Using B, p to end.
ROW 5: K0 (2:5:7) B, [work across 5th row of 20sts patt rep] 3 times, work first 4sts of 5th row of patt rep, then k3 (5:8:10) B.
ROW 6: P3 (5:8:10) B, work last 4sts of 6th row of patt rep, [work across 6th row of 20sts patt rep] 3 times, p0 (2:5:7) B.
These 2 rows set chart 2.
Cont in patt to end of chart 2.
Cont in yarn A. Cont in st st until back measures 19(21:23½:26)in (48(54:60:66)cm) from cast-on edge, ending with a p row.

Shape shoulders
Cast off 5sts at beg of next 2 rows. (57 (61:67:71) sts)
Cast off 7sts at beg of foll 2 rows. (43 (47:53:57) sts)

◄ This dress is knitted in Debbie Bliss Rialto Aran in A: 029 Mid Grey, B: 035 Blossom, C: 010 Lime, and D: 038 Royal.

Cast off 7 (8:10:11) sts at beg of foll 2 rows. (29 (31:33:35) sts)
Leave rem sts on a stitch holder.

Front

Work as given for back until front measures 16½(19:21:23)in (42(48:54:59)cm) from cast-on edge, ending with a p row.

Shape neck

NEXT ROW: K23 (24:26:27) sts, turn and work on these sts only for first side of front neck, leave rem sts on a spare needle.
NEXT ROW: P to end.
NEXT ROW: K to last 3sts, k2tog, k1.
Rep the last 2 rows 3 times more. (19 (20:22:23) sts)
Work straight until front measures the same as back to shoulder, with a WS row.

Shape shoulders

Cast off 5sts at beg of next row. (14 (15:17:18) sts)
Work 1 row.
Cast off 7 sts at beg of next row. (7 (8:10:11) sts)

Work 1 row.
Cast off rem 7 (8:10:11) sts.
With RS facing, slip center 21 (23:25:27) sts onto a stitch holder, rejoin yarn to rem sts, k to end.
NEXT ROW: P to end.
NEXT ROW: K1, skpo, k to end.
Rep the last 2 rows 3 times more. (19 (20:22:23) sts)
Work straight until front measures the same as back to shoulder, ending with a RS row.

Cast off 5sts at beg of next row. (14 (15:17:18) sts)
Work 1 row.
Cast off 7 sts at beg of next row.
Work 1 row.
Cast off rem 7 (8:10:11) sts.

Sleeves (make 2)

Using needles A and yarn B, cast on 34 (38:38:42) sts.
ROW 1 RIB: K2, [p2, k2] to end.
Cut off B. Join in yarn A.
ROW 2 RIB: P2, [k2, p2] to end.
Rep the last 2 rows 4 times more, using yarn A only, inc 3 (1:3:1) sts evenly across last row. (37 (39:41:43) sts)

Change to needles B and beg with a k row cont in st st.
Work 2 rows.
Work from chart 1 as foll:
ROW 1: K1 (2:3:4) in yarn A, work last 2sts of 1st row of patt rep, [work across 1st row of 8 st patt rep] 4 times, work st 1 of 1st row of patt rep, k1 (2:3:4) A.
ROW 2: P1 (2:3:4) A, work st 1 of 2nd row of patt rep, [work across 2nd row of 8 st patt rep] 4 times, work last 2sts of 2nd row of patt rep, p1 (2:3:4) A.
These 2 rows set chart 1.
Cont in patt to end of chart 1.
Cont in A.
NEXT ROW: P to end, inc 1 st at center of row. (38 (40:42:44) sts)
INC ROW: K3, M1, k to last 3 sts, M1, k3.
Work 5 rows.
Rep the last 6 rows 1 (2:3:4) times more and the inc row again. (44 (48:52:56) sts)
Work from chart 2 as foll:
ROW 1: Using yarn A, k to end.

ROW 2: Using yarn B, p to end.
ROW 3: Using A, k to end.
ROW 4: Using B, p to end.
ROW 5: K10 (12:14:16) in yarn B, work across 5th row of 20sts patt rep, work first 4 sts of 5th row of patt rep, k10 (12:14:16) B.
ROW 6: P10 (12:14:16) B, work last 4 sts of 6th row of patt rep, work across 6th row of 20sts patt rep, p10 (12:14:16) B.
These 2 rows set chart 2.
Cont in patt to end of chart 2, then cont in A. At the same time, inc 1 st at each end of the next and 2 (2:3:3) foll 6th rows. (50 (54:60:64) sts)
Cont even until sleeve measures 9½(11½:13½:15)in (24(29:34:38)cm) from cast-on edge, ending with a p row.
Cast off.

Neckband

Join right shoulder seam.
With RS facing, using needles A and yarn A, pick up and k 14(16:16:18) sts down LS of front neck, k across 21(23:25:27) sts from front neck, pick up and k14 (16:16:18) sts up RS of front neck, k across 29 (31:33:35) sts from back neck. (78 (86:90:98) sts)
ROW 1: K2, [p2, k2] to end.
ROW 2: P2, [k2, p2] to end.
Rep these 2 rows twice.
Cut off A. Join in B. Work row 1 again.
Cast off in rib.

Finishing

Join left shoulder and neckband seam. Matching center of cast-off edge of sleeve to shoulder, sew in sleeves. Join side and sleeve seams.

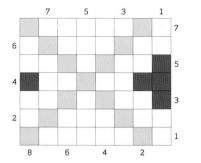

Chart 1

Key
☐ A: Mid Grey
▨ C: Lime
■ D: Royal

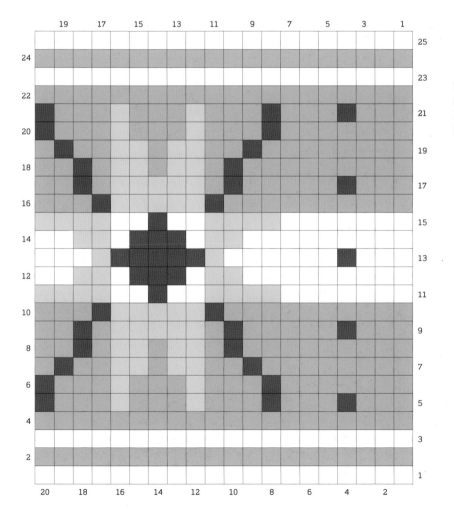

Chart 2

Key
☐ A: Mid grey
▨ B: Blossom
▨ C: Lime
■ D: Royal

To make
these projects, from
left to right, see pages
20–23, 48–51,
40–43

top tip

If you prefer, swap the stalk here for a multicolored pom-pom (see p.244).

Child's beanie hat

Embrace a world of color with this fall-hued striped hat. In simple stockinette stitch with a mini garter-stitch brim, you'll see this beanie grow fast. What's more, it's small enough to make a perfect starter project for someone who's not tackled colors before.

❋ you will need

DIFFICULTY Moderate

SIZE To fit a child age 4 years and upward

YARN
Rico Merino Aran 50g and Debbie Bliss Cashmerino Aran 50g

A x 1   B x 1   C x 1   D x 1

NEEDLES
1 pair of US8 (5mm/UK6) needles

GAUGE
18sts and 24 rows over 4in (10cm) square in st st

NOTIONS
Darning needle

◀ This beanie is knitted in Debbie Bliss Rialto Aran in A: 001 Stone, B: 042 Sienna, and D: 010 Lime; and Debbie Bliss Cashmerino Aran in C: Amber.

How to make

Brim
Using yarn C, cast on 80sts.
Work 3 rows in g st.
Cont in st st working in stripes as follows:
ROWS 1–2: Yarn A.
ROWS 3–4: Yarn B.
ROWS 5–6: Yarn A.
ROWS 7–8: Yarn C.
Rep these 8 rows until work measures 4in (10cm).

Crown
Keep stripe sequence work as follows:
ROW 1: [K5, k2tog] x 11, k3. (69sts)
ROWS 2–4: St st.
ROW 5: [K4, k2tog] x 11, k3. (58sts)
ROWS 6–8: St st.
ROW 9: [K3, k2tog] x 11, k3. (47sts)
ROWS 10–12: St st.
ROW 13: [K2, k2tog] x 11, k3. (36sts)
ROWS 14–16: St st.
ROW 17: [K1, k2tog] x 12. (24sts)
ROWS 18–20: St st.
ROW 21: K2tog to end. (12sts)
Break off yarn, thread through rem sts, and draw up loosely.
Sew the seam using a darning needle.

Stalk
With yarn D, cast on 10sts.
Work 5½in (14cm) st st.
Cast off.
With RS of st st outside, roll up row ends tightly and secure with pins.
Sew row ends in place to secure.
Push through top of hat and secure, pull thread through sts, and fasten off tightly.

Child's striped scarf

A fun foray into the world of color is this pom-pom-trimmed, garter stitch scarf featuring stripes of four different-colored yarns. In fact, this project is a great way to use up leftovers, since you can choose to do the stripes and the pom-poms in any coordinating colors.

❄ you will need

DIFFICULTY Easy

SIZE To fit a child age 3–4 years, 5 x 37in (12 x 96cm)

YARN
Debbie Bliss Rialto
Aran 50g

A x 1   **B** x 1   **C** x 1   **D** x 1

NEEDLES
1 pair of US8 (5mm/UK6) needles

GAUGE
19sts and 36 rows over 4in (10cm) in g st

NOTIONS
Darning needle
Cardboard (for pom-poms)

◄ This scarf is knitted in Rico Essentials Soft Merino Aran in A: 042 Sienna, B: 106 Ecru, C: 042 Sunshine, and D: 010 Lime.

How to make

When working narrow stripes, twist the yarns around each other at the edges of the scarf when changing to a new color, being careful not to pull them too tightly. Over wider stripes, you may find it looks neater to cut the yarn first and join in the new color (see p.185), leaving an 8in (20cm) tail of each yarn to sew in later.

With yarn A, cast on 22sts.

ROWS 1–10: Work in g st (k every st on every row).

ROWS 11–12: K in yarn B.

ROWS 13–14: K in yarn A.

ROWS 15–24: K in yarn B.

ROWS 25–26: K in yarn C.

ROWS 27–28: K in yarn B.

ROWS 29–38: K in yarn C.

ROWS 39–40: K in yarn D.

ROWS 41–42: K in yarn C.

ROWS 43–52: K in yarn D.

ROWS 53–54: K in yarn A.

ROWS 55–56: K in yarn D.

These 56 rows form the stripe rep.

Rep the stripe rep 6 times.

K 10 rows in yarn A.

Cast off. Then sew in yarn ends.

Making small pom-poms

Unlike bigger pom-poms (see p.244), here we need 6 small pom-poms: 4 in yarn A and 2 in yarn C. Take a piece of cardboard 6in x ¾in (15cm x 1.5cm) and cut a slit in the center of both ends. Lay 8in (20cm) of yarn along the card and secure in the slit at each end. Wrap the remaining length of the yarn around the cardboard widthwise about 100 times. Free the length of yarn from the slits and slip the wrapped yarn off the cardboard, taking the strand of yarn with it. Tie the two ends of the length of yarn together tightly, bringing the wrapped yarn around to form a circle. Cut the loops at the outer edge then trim into shape.

Fuzzy finishes The pom-poms add great tactile interest here, but tassels will also work well.

Child's cowl hood

Knitting the pieces of this snuggly cowl is simple and, since it uses a chunky yarn, you'll see it knits up fast. To put a twist on a normal cowl, and make it child-friendly for all weathers, a hood is created by joining the pieces together and casting off on three needles.

❄ you will need

DIFFICULTY Easy

SIZE To fit a child, age 3–4 years

YARN
Rowan Big Wool
100g

A x 1

NEEDLES
A: 1 pair of US17 (12mm) needles or 24in (60cm) long US17 (12mm) circular needle
B: Spare US17 (12mm) needle

GAUGE
8.5sts and 12 rows over 4in (10cm) in st st

NOTIONS
1 x 1½in (40mm) button
Darning needle

How to make

First front flap
Cast on 10sts.
Work 6 rows in g st, (k to end of every row).
  Make buttonhole.
ROW 7: K3, yo, k2tog, k to end.
Work 5 rows in g st.
Leave sts on needle.
To ensure that the buttonhole is not too big, pull yarn firmly after k2tog to shorten the yo and surrounding sts.

Second front flap
Cast on 10sts.
Work 12 rows in g st.
Leave sts on needle.

Front band
K across 10sts of second front flap, using cable cast on (see p180), cast on 54sts, k across 10sts of first front flap. (74sts)
Work 5 rows in g st.

Hood
ROW 1 (RS): K to end.
ROW 2: K10, p54, k10.

Rep these 2 rows until work measures 11in (27cm) from cast-on edge of front band.
Fold work in half RS together, 37sts either side and, taking a third needle, cast off one stitch from each needle together to close the back of the hood—a three-needle cast-off (see p.189).

Finishing
Weave in the yarn ends, block (see p.238), and sew the button in place.

Contrasting stitches The garter stitch edge to the hood matches the snuggly "scarf" that extends from the flaps.

➤ This hood is knitted in Rowan Big Wool 026 Blue Velvet.

top tip

You can use this method
of knitting ties instead of
an I-cord (see p.75) to
join mittens.

Child's hat with ear flaps

Hats are cozy but hats with ear flaps are the ultimate way to keep warm. For this piece, you knit the flaps first then join them together and knit the hat. The simple decreases used here in the shaping of the crown create a detail that leads your eye to the pom-pom on top.

❄ you will need

DIFFICULTY Moderate

SIZE To fit a child age 8–10 years

YARN
Debbie Bliss Cashmerino Aran 50g

A x 2, plus scraps of yarn for the pom-pom

NEEDLES
1 pair of US8 (5mm/UK6) needles

GAUGE
20sts and 25 rows over 4in (10cm) in st st

NOTIONS
Darning needle

◄ This hat is knitted in Debbie Bliss Cashmerino Aran in 502 Lime.

How to make

Not all rows in the flaps are worked to the end. Turn work where indicated.

Left flap
Cast on 33sts.
ROW 1: P.
ROW 2: [P1, k1] x 12, p1, turn.
ROW 3: S1, k24.
ROW 4: [P1, k1] x 11, p1, turn.
ROW 5: S1, k22.
ROW 6: [P1, k1] x 10, p1, turn.
ROW 7: S1, k20.
Cont to foll patt as set, dec the st worked on each row until:
ROW 25: S1, k2.
Put this ear flap aside.

Right flap
Cast on 33sts.
ROW 1: P.
ROW 2: [K1, p1] x 16, k1.
ROW 3: K25, turn.
ROW 4: S1, [k1, p1] x 12.
ROW 5: K23, turn.
ROW 6: S1, [k1, p1] x 11.
ROW 7: K21, turn.
Cont to foll patt as set, dec the st worked on each row until:
ROW 26: S1, k1, p1, cast on an extra 37sts and turn this piece around. Pick up the left ear flap and, using the yarn you just cast on with, work the

left ear flap as foll: [p1, k1] x 16, p1. This has joined the two pieces tog with a section of new sts in the middle.
ROW 27 (RS): K33, p37, k33. (103sts)
ROW 28: [P1, k1] x 51, p1.
ROW 29: K.
ROWS 30–35: Rep rows 28–29 three times.
ROW 36: P.
ROW 37: K.
ROWS 38–55: Rep rows 36–37 nine times.
ROW 56: P2, [p2tog, p23] x 4, p1. (99sts)
ROW 57: K1, [k2tog, k22] x 4, k2. (95sts)
ROW 58: P2, [p2tog, p21] x 4, p1. (91sts)
ROW 59: K1, [k2tog, k20] x 4, k2. (87sts)
ROW 60: P2, [p2tog, p19] x 4, p1. (83sts)
Foll patt as set, dec every row as shown, until:
ROW 76: P2, [p2tog, p3] x 4, p1. (19sts)
ROW 77: [S1, k2tog, psso] x 6, k1. (7sts)

Finishing
Pass the yarn through all rem st and draw them tog. With right sides facing, use this end to sew a neat whipstitch (see p.240) down the back seam. To make the ties, cast on 50sts, then immediately cast these 50sts off again. Make two ties and sew each to the points of ear flaps. Make a pom-pom and sew to the top of hat.

To make
these projects, from
left to right, see pages
62–63, 70–73,
54–55

Sheep scarf with pockets

What child could resist plunging her hands into the pockets of this adorable scarf? This monochrome project combines intarsia with different stitch techniques to create a 3-D effect in the sheep's face on the finished scarf. You can adjust the length of the scarf to fit your child.

 ## you will need

DIFFICULTY Moderate

SIZE To fit a child age 3–6 years

YARN
Malabrigo Rastita 50g

A x 4   **B** x 1

NEEDLES
A: 1 pair of US6 (4mm/UK8) needles
B: 1 pair of US7 (4.5mm/UK7) needles

GAUGE
19sts and 41 rows over 4in (10cm) in g st on US7 (4.5mm/UK7) needles

NOTIONS
2 black buttons for nostrils
Darning needle

How to make

Scarf
Using yarn A and needles B, cast on 21sts.

Head-end increase shaping
ROW 1: K.
ROW 2: K1, inc 1 (kfb), knit to end. (22sts)
ROWS 3-10: K1, inc 1st (kfb), k to end. (30sts)
ROW 11: S1, k to end.
ROW 12: S1, k to end.
Rep rows 11–12 until the scarf measures 48in (1.2m) long. (Adjust the length of the scarf by increasing or reducing rows here, to suit the height of the child.)

Tail-end decrease shaping
NEXT ROW: K to last 3 sts, k2tog, k1. (29sts)
Repeat the last row 8 times. (21sts)
Cast off.

Pockets
Both pockets are knitted from the top edge downward using a cable cast-on to give a firm edge (see p. 180). Knitting the patterned head pocket first means that you can adjust the rows of the plain tail pocket to match any difference in length that may occur due to stitch gauge variation in the intarsia. The black (face) st st will work up slightly longer than the cream (background) g stitch.

◀ This scarf is made with Malabrigo Rastita in A: 63 Natural and B: 195 Black.

Head pocket

Using yarn A and needles A, cast on 30sts using cable cast-on.

ROW 1: *K1, p1; rep from * to end.
Rep row 1 three times.

Change to needles B, and working pocket in intarsia technique, follow colors and k/p st as shown on chart:.

ROW 1: K in yarn A.

ROW 2: S1, k to end in A.
Cont as per chart.

Where colors meet, wrap yarns on the WS. When this occurs between knit and purl stitches, bring knit stitch yarn between the needles to the side facing you, and wrap the purl yarn under it before working the purl stitch. When between a purl and a knit stitch, wrap the knit stitch yarn under the purl stitch yarn before taking it back between the needles and working the knit stitch.

Work eyes in straight intarsia, or weave black behind white stitches as for Fair Isle knitting.

ROW 31: S1, work as chart to last 3sts, k2tog, k1. (29sts)
Repeat the last row 8 times, working color and stitches as shown in the chart. (21sts)

ROWS 40–41: K in yarn A.
Cast off.

Tail pocket

With needles A and yarn A, cast on 30sts using cable cast on.

ROW 1: *K1, p1; rep from * to end.
Rep row 1 3 times.
Change to needles B.

ROW 5: S1, k to end.
Rep last row 41 times.

ROW 47: K to last 3sts, k2tog, k1. (29sts)
Rep last row 8 times. (21sts)

ROW 56: K.

ROW 57: K.
Cast off.

Ears (make 2)

Using yarn B and needles A, cast on 10sts.

ROW 1: K1, kfb, k to end.

ROW 2: K.
Rep rows 1 and 2 twice. (13sts).

ROW 7: K.

ROW 8: K.

ROW 9: K1, k2tog, k to end.

ROW 10: K.
Rep rows 9 and 10 twice. (10sts).
Cast off.

Face close-up Here you can see the intarsia knitting in detail and the embellishments that create the face.

Finishing

Carefully sew the ends of the
intarsia knitting into the back of
the head pocket.

Embroider the pupils and mouth, and
attach the buttons for the nostrils.
Make sure these are well secured.
Using a darning needle, run a thread
of yarn through the stitches
of the shaped end of the ears, and
pull taut, gathering it into an ear
shape. Do the same with the short,
straight end, and sew the ears to
the sides of the head.

Block the pieces (see p.238). While
doing this, ease the length of the
pockets to match, and the width of
both pockets to match that of the
scarf. Try not to flatten the ears while
doing this.

Lay the head pocket onto the head
end of the scarf, and carefully
matching the rows, sew the pocket
onto the scarf. If you can use the
cast-on and cast-off yarn tails for
this, it will save you from having to
sew them in separately.

Do the same with the tail pocket at
the other end of the scarf.

Chart

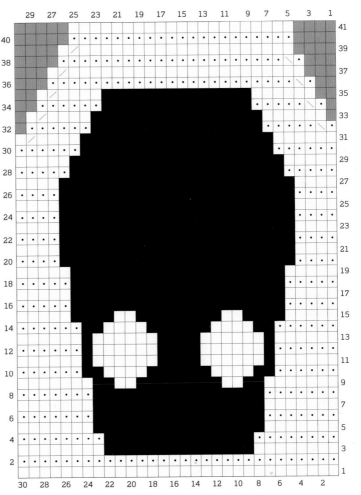

Key

☐ A: Natural
■ B: Black
☐ Knit on RS, purl on WS
⊡ Purl on RS, knit on WS

Hooded scarf

The multicolored, chunky yarn used in this pattern knits up really quickly, and the wool content ensures it is a snugly warm scarf to wear. A simple-to-follow, two-stitch basketweave pattern makes the most of this effective yarn.

✳ you will need

DIFFICULTY Moderate

SIZE To fit a child age 4 years and up

YARN
Lorna's Laces Shepard 100g

A x 3

NEEDLES
1 pair of US10 (6mm/UK4) needles

GAUGE
18sts and 22 rows over 4in (10cm) in patt

NOTIONS
Darning needle

How to make

Hood

Cast on 42sts.
Work 2 rows in st st.
ROW 1: K2, *p2, k2, rep from * to end of row.
ROW 2: P2, *k2, p2, rep from * to end of row.
ROW 3: P2, *k2, p2, rep from * to end of row.
ROW 4: K2, *p2, k2, rep from * to end of row.
Rep rows 1–4 until work measures 18in (45cm).
Work 2 rows in st st.
Cast off.
Fold hood in half and join back seam.
Fold back 1½in (4cm) from edge and catch down at edges.

Scarf

Cast on 6sts.
Work in patt as for hood.
At the same time, inc 1 st at each end of every row, working increased sts into the patt, until there are 26sts.
Cont in patt until work measures 43in (110cm).
Keeping continuity of patt, dec 1 st at each end of every row until there are 6sts.
Cast off.
Make 3 pom-poms (see p.244).

Finishing

Sew scarf edge to bottom edge of hood. Sew pom-poms to scarf ends and to tip of hood.

> This scarf hood is knitted in Lorna's Laces Shepard Bulky.

❄ you will need

DIFFICULTY Moderate

SIZE To fit a child age
2–3 (3–4:4–5) years

YARN
Debbie Bliss Rialto DK 50g

A x 1   B x 1

NEEDLES
4 x US6 (4mm/UK8) double-
pointed needles

GAUGE
22sts and 30 rows over
4in (10cm) in st st

NOTIONS
Small stitch holder
Stitch markers x 2
Darning needle

SPECIAL ABBREVIATIONS
PM Place marker.
SM Slip marker.

Child's easy mittens

Hands will always be warm with this pair of connected mittens; simply feed the cord through the sleeves of a coat or warm sweater. This project is an ideal way to practice knitting "in the round" since, aside from the rib, it only uses knit stitches and simple shaping.

How to make

Mittens (make 2)

Using yarn A, cast on 30 (32:34) sts plus 1 extra st and share between three needles. To "join in the round," slip the extra stitch to the left needle and then knit first and last stitches together before following the pattern. Work k1, p1 rib for 2 rounds. Change to yarn B.
Cont in k1, p1 rib for 12 (14:16) rounds.
Cont in st st (k every round).
Round 1: k to last st, M1, k1 (31 (33:35) sts)
K 2 rounds.

Shape thumb

K15 (16:17) sts, PM, M1, k1, M1, PM, k15 (16:17) sts. (33 (35:37) sts)
K 1 round.
K15 (16:17) sts, SM, M1, k3, M1, SM, k15 (16:17) sts. (35 (37:39) sts)
K 1 round.
K15 (16:17) sts, SM, M1, k5, M1, SM, k15 (16:17) sts. (37 (39:41) sts)
K 1 round.
K15 (16:17) sts, SM, M1, k7, M1, SM, k15 (16:17) sts. (39 (41:43) sts)
K 1 round.

◄ These mittens use Debbie Bliss
Rialto DK in A: 44 Aqua and
B: 12 Red.

K15 (16:17) sts, SM, M1, k9, M1, SM, k15 (16:17) sts. (41 (43:45) sts)
K 1 round.
K15 (16:17) sts, SM, M1, k11, M1, SM, k 15 (16:17) sts. (43 (45:47) sts)
K 1 round.
K15 (16:17) sts, remove markers, and place 13 thumb sts onto stitch holder, k to end of round. (30 (32:34) sts)
K every round for 1¼(1½:2)in (3(4:5)cm), knitting across thumb gusset.

Shape mitten top

ROUND 1: *K2, k2tog, k2, rep from * to last 0 (2:4) sts, k0 (2:4). (25 (27:29) sts)
ROUND 2: K.
ROUND 3: *K2tog, k1, rep from * to last 1 (0:2) sts, k1 (0:2). (17 (18:20) sts)
ROUND 4: K.
ROUND 5: *K2tog, rep from * to last 1 (0:0) sts, k1 (0:0). (9 (9:10) sts)
Break yarn, thread through stitches, pull tightly, and finish off.

Thumb

Using yarn B, place 13sts from stitch holder onto two needles, and, with the third needle, pick up, and k 4sts

across gusset gap. (17sts)
K 6 (8:10) rounds.

Shape thumb top

*K1, k2tog; rep from * to last 2sts, k2tog. (11sts)
Break the yarn, thread through the stitches, pull tightly, and finish off. Sew in the ends of the yarn using a darning needle.

I-cord

Using yarn A and two dpns, cast on 3sts. Knit one row. Instead of turning the work around, slide all the stitches to the other end of the needle they're on, and swap needle to left hand. With RS facing, knit into the first stitch pulling the yarn firmly across the back of the stitches (it's attached at the left side of the work). Tug the yarn again to pull the knitting around into a tube and complete the row. Repeat until the I-cord measures approx 37(39:41in (96(100:104)cm) long (to fit up sleeve, across back, and down sleeve). Attach the cord to each mitten.

Ear warmer headband

When it's fresh outside but not chilly enough for a wool hat, this knitted headband is just the thing to keep ears warm. Measure your child's head before you start, so you know how many cable repeats to knit; in fact, measure your head and knit a matching one for yourself.

❄ you will need

DIFFICULTY Easy/moderate

SIZE To fit a child age 8–10 years

YARN
Debbie Bliss Rialto Aran 50g

A x 1

NEEDLES
A: 1 pair of US8 (5mm/UK6) needles
B: Cable needle

GAUGE
18sts and 24 rows over 4in (10cm) in st st

NOTIONS
2 buttons
Darning needle

SPECIAL ABBREVIATIONS
C4B (Cross 4 back): Slip 2sts to cable needle (cn) and hold at back of work, k2 from LH needle then k2 from cn.
C4F (Cross 4 front): Slip next 2sts to cn and hold at front of work, k2 from LH needle then k2 from cn.

◄ This headband is knitted in Debbie Bliss Rialto Aran in 029 Mid Grey.

How to make

Cast on 14sts. Leave a long yarn tail to sew the buttons on with later.

ROWS 1–4: K.

ROW 5 (RS): K2, C4B, k8.

ROW 6 AND EVERY FOLL ALT ROW UNLESS OTHERWISE SPECIFIED: K2, p4, k2, p4, k2.

ROW 7: K.

ROW 9: As row 5.

ROW 11: K8, C4F, k2.

ROW 13: K.

ROW 15: As row 11.

Rows 5–16 is one repeat. Work as many repeats as you need to fit snugly around your child's head. (To increase the length of this headband by a small amount, work an extra 2 rows of g st at the start and the finish. For a longer alteration, if adding one complete cable pattern doesn't work out to the correct length, try adding rows between the cable crossovers in combination with the first method.)

There are 9 more repeats in this patt.

NEXT RS ROW: K2, cast off 4sts, k1, cast off 4sts, k1.

NEXT ROW: K2, cast on 4sts, k2, cast on 4sts, k2.

Cast off knitwise and weave in the ends. Sew on 2 buttons.

▲ The pink headband is knitted in Debbie Bliss Rialto Aran in 035 Blossom.

To make these projects, from left to right, see pages 96–97, 130–131, 100–101, 74–75, 70–73

Projects for
Women

top tip

Casting on with the pink yarn gives a sophisticated design detail to the ribs.

Easy Fair Isle sweater

This simple-shaped sweater is an ideal Fair Isle starter project, as it combines this traditional technique of color patterning with easy-to-work stripes. The Fair Isle patterns have short floats, so there is no need to weave them in at the back of the work.

✳ you will need

DIFFICULTY Moderate

SIZE To fit an adult woman
S (M:L)

YARN
Rowan Felted Tweed
DK 50g

A x 9 (10:11) **B** x 2 (3:3)

C x 2 (2:2) **D** x 2 (2:2) **E** x 2 (3:3)

NEEDLES
A: 1 pair US6 (4mm/UK8)
needles
B: 1 pair US7 (4.5mm/UK7)
needles
C: 20in (50cm) long US6 (4mm/
UK8) circular needle

GAUGE
21sts and 25 rows over 4in
(10cm) in patt on US7 (4.5mm/
UK7) needles

NOTIONS
2 stitch holders
Darning needle

SPECIAL ABBREVIATIONS
M1P (Make 1st purlwise): Pick up
loop before next st and slip it
onto LH needle, p this st.

How to make

Back
Using needles A and yarn E, cast on
101 (113:125) sts.
Change to yarn A.
ROW 1 (RS): K2, *p1, k2; rep from *
to end.
ROW 2: P2, *k1, p2; rep from * to end.
Cont to work in rib until you have
completed 7 rows, ending on a RS row.
NEXT ROW (WS): P1, M1P, p to last st,
M1P, p1. (103 (115:127) sts)
Change to needles B and beg with
a k row as shown in row 1 of the
chart. Work in st st in patt, stranding
yarn not in use loosely across the
WS of work.
Read chart on p.84 from right to left
on RS (k) rows and from left to right
on WS (p) rows. Both RS and WS rows
will start and end with stitch 1 in the
chart. Cont until you have completed
3 full patt reps plus rows 1–4,
ending on a WS row.
Cont to work in stripe patt as foll:
4 rows in A, 2 rows in E, 4 rows in A,
2 rows in B, 4 rows in A, 2 rows in C,

4 rows in A, and 2 rows in D.
**Rep these 24 rows. At the same
time, when the work measures
14 (14½:15½)in (35 (37:39)cm) from
beg, ending on a WS row.**

Shape armholes
Cont in stripe patt as written above.
Cast off 4 (5:6) sts at beg of next
2 rows. (95 (105:115) sts)
ROWS 3, 5, 7, AND 9: K1, skpo, k to last
3sts. K2tog, k1.
ROWS 4 AND 6: P1, p2tog tbl, p to last
3sts, p2tog, p1.
ROW 8: P.
(83 (93:103) sts)
Cont without shaping until the
armhole measures 8(9¼:9½)in
(21(23:24)cm) ending with a WS row.

Shape back neck and shoulders
Cont working in stripe patt as set,
k across 27 (29:31) sts, turn, leave
rem sts on a spare needle and work
each side separately.

◄ This sweater uses Rowan Felted
Tweed DK, in A: 173 Duck Egg, B: 178
Seasalter, C: 181 Mineral, D: 151
Bilberry, and E: 150 Rage.

Chart

Read all odd number (RS) rows from right to left, and all even number (WS) rows from left to right.

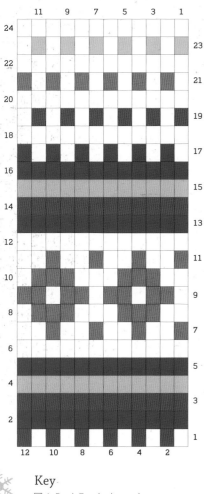

Key

☐ A: Duck Egg (pale gray)
■ B: Seasalter (deep blue)
☐ C: Mineral (gold)
■ D: Bilberry (purple)
☐ E: Rage (guava pink)

ROW 1 (WS): P1, p2tog, p to end of row.
ROW 2: K to last 3sts, k2tog, k1.
ROW 3: Rep row 1. (24 (26:28) sts)
Cast off.
With RS facing, slip the center 29 (35:41) sts to a holder for the back neck. Rejoin yarn to rem 27 (29:31) sts and k to end of row.
ROW 1: P to last 3sts, p2tog tbl, p1.
ROW 2: K 1, skpo, k to end.
ROW 3: Rep row 1. Cast off.

Front

Work as for the back until the work measures 4in (10cm) less than the back, ending on a WS row.

Shape front neck

Keeping the striped patt as set, k across 34 (38:42) sts, turn, leave rem sts on a spare needle and work each side separately.
ROW 1 (WS): Cast off 2 (2:3) sts at beg of row, p to end.
ROW 2: K to last 3sts, k2tog, k1.
ROW 3: Rep row 1.
ROW 4: Rep row 2.
ROW 5: P1, p2tog, p to end of row.
Rep row 4 and row 5 until 24 (26:28) sts rem.
Cont without shaping until the front matches to the back shoulder, ending on a WS row. Cast off.
With RS facing, slip center 15 (17:19) sts to stitch holder for the center front. Rejoin yarn to rem 34 (38:42) sts and k to end of row.
ROW 1 (WS): P to last 3sts, p2tog tbl, p1.
ROW 2: Cast off 2 (2:3) sts at beg of row, k to end.

ROW 3: Rep row 1.
ROW 4: Rep row 2.
ROW 5: Rep row 1.
ROW 6: K1, skpo, k to end.
Rep rows 5 and 6 until 24 (26:28) sts rem. Complete to match first side.

Sleeves (make 2)

Using needles A and yarn E, cast on 47 (50:53) sts.
Change to yarn A and work in rib as written for the back for 11 rows.
1st and 3rd sizes only
NEXT ROW (WS): P1, M1P, p to last st, M1P, p1. (49 (55) sts)
2nd size only
NEXT ROW (WS): P1, M1P, p to end. (51sts)
All sizes
Change to needles B and starting at row 1, work from the chart until you have completed rows 1–4.
RS rows will start with stitch 1 in the chart and end with stitch 1 (3:1). WS rows will start with stitch 1 (3:1) in the chart and end with stitch 1.
ROW 5 (RS): Using yarn B, k1 M1, k to last st, M1, k1.
Cont with patt, until 24 rows of patt are completed, then cont working in yarn A without any pattern.
At the same time, inc 1 st at each end of every foll 6th row until there are 67 (71:77) sts; then on every foll 8th row until there are 77 (81:87) sts.
Cont without shaping until the sleeve measures 17¾ (18:18½)in (45 (46:47)cm) from cast-on edge, ending on a WS row.

Shape sleeve head

Cast off 4 (5:6) sts at beg of next
2 rows. (69 (71:75) sts)

NEXT ROW: K1, skpo, k to last 3sts,
k2tog, k1.

NEXT ROW: P1, p2tog, p to last 3sts,
p2tog tbl, p1.

Rep last 2 rows twice more.
(57 (59:63) sts)

Cast off 8 (8:9) sts at beg of next
6 rows. Cast off rem 9 (11:9) sts.

Neckband

Join shoulder seams.

Using needle C and yarn A, with RS
facing and beg at left shoulder, pick
up and k26 evenly down the left front
neck, k across 15 (17:19) sts from
front neck holder, then pick up and
k26 evenly up the right front neck to
the shoulder seam, pick up and k3
evenly do wn the back neck, k across
29 (35:41) sts from back neck holder,
then pick up and k3 to the shoulder.
(102 (110:118) sts)

ROUND 1: P.

ROUND 2: K.

Rep rounds 1 and 2.

2nd size only

Inc 1st at end of last round. (111sts)

3rd size only

Dec 1st at end of last round. (117sts)

All sizes

ROUND 5: *K2, p1; rep from * to end.

Work in rib as set for 6 rounds.
Change to yarn E and work 1 round.
Cast off loosely in rib.

Making up

Sew in all loose ends with a large-eyed needle. Join
side and sleeve seams, being careful to match the
pattern. With the center of the sleeve matching
the shoulder seam, sew in the sleeve. Block lightly
(see p.238) according to the yarn's ballband.

This sweater is knitted in
Rowan Pure Wool DK in
A: 00030 Damson and
B: 00019 Avocado.

Cable and bobble sweater

This richly textured classic winter knit incorporates a cable and bobble panel on the front and the back of the sweater. The roll detail and accent color at the neck and rib edges gives this sweater immense style. It's almost a case of the stronger the contrast, the better.

❄ you will need

DIFFICULTY Moderate

SIZE To fit an adult woman S(M:L)

YARN Rowan Pure Wool DK 50g

A x 9(10:11)   **B** x 1(1:1)

NEEDLES
A: 1 pair of US4 (3.5mm) needles
B: 1 pair of US6 (4mm/UK8) needles
C: 20in (50cm) long US 4 (3.5mm) circular needle
D: Cable needle

GAUGE
20sts and 30 rows over 4in (10cm) worked in st st on US6 (4mm/UK8) needles

NOTIONS
2 stitch holders
Darning needle

SPECIAL ABBREVIATIONS
C4B (Cross 4 Back): S2 to cable needle (cn) and hold at back, k2 from LH needle then k2 from cn.
C4F (Cross 4 Front): S2 to cn and hold at front, k2 from LH needle then k2 from cn.
MB (Make bobble): K into front, back, and front of next st, turn and k3, turn and p3, turn and k3, turn and s1, k2tog, psso.

How to make

Back

Using needles A and yarn B, cast on 120(126:132) sts.

ROW 1 (RS): K.

ROW 2: P.

Change to yarn A.

ROW 3: K 1 row.

ROW 4: P1, k1, *p2, k1; rep from * to last st, p1.

ROW 5: K1, p1, * k2, p1; rep from * to last st, k1.

Rep rows 4–5 until the rib measures 2½in (6cm) from beg, ending on a WS row.

Change to needles B and cont in patt as foll:

ROW 1 (RS): K24 (27:30) sts, p2, [k8, p7] x 4, k8, p2, k24 (27:30) sts.

ROW 2 AND EVERY FOLL ALT ROW: P24 (27:30) sts, k2, [p8, k7] x 4, p8, k2, p24 (27:30) sts.

ROW 3: Rep row 1.

ROW 5: K24 (27:30) sts, p2, [C4B, C4F, p3, MB, p3] x 4, C4B, C4F, p2, k24 (27:30) sts.

ROW 7 AND ROW 9: Rep row 1.

ROW 11: K24 (27:30) sts, p2, [C4B, C4F, p7] x 4, C4B, C4F, p2, k24 (27:30) sts.

ROW 12: Rep row 2.

Rep these 12 rows until the work measures 15(15½:16)in (38(39:40)cm) from beg, ending on a WS row.

Shape armholes

Keeping patt correct throughout, cast off 7 (7:8) sts at beg of next 2 rows. (106 (112:116) sts)

NEXT ROW: K1, skpo, patt to last 3sts, k2tog, k1.

NEXT ROW: P1, p2tog, patt to last 3sts, p2tog tbl, p1.

Rep last 2 rows 3 times, then first again. (92 (98:102) sts)

Cont without shaping until the armhole measures 8(8¼:9)in (20(21:23)cm) from beg of shaping, ending with a WS row.

This beautiful design features a braided cable stitch that alternates with a panel of bobbles to create an interesting, raised texture.

Back neck and shoulder shaping

(RS facing) Keeping patt correct, cast off 13 (14:15) sts, patt until you have 14 (15:15) sts on the RH needle, turn, leave rem sts on a spare needle and work each side separately.

NEXT ROW (WS): Dec 1 st at beg of row, patt to end of row.

NEXT ROW: Cast off rem 13 (14:14) sts. With RS facing, slip center 38 (40:42) sts to stitch holder. Rejoin yarn and patt to end of row.

NEXT ROW (WS): Cast off 13 (14:15) sts at beg of row, patt to last 2 sts, p2tog.

NEXT ROW: Cast off rem 13 (14:14) sts.

Front

Work as for the back until the armhole measures 4¼(5:5½)in (11(12:14)cm) from beg of shaping, ending on a WS row.

Front neck shaping

NEXT ROW (RS): Patt across 36 (38:39) sts, turn, leave rem sts on a spare needle and work each side separately. Dec 1 st at neck edge on the next 5 (5:7) rows. (31 (33:32) sts) Then cont on every foll alt row until 26 (28:29) sts rem.

Cont without shaping until the front matches the back to shoulder, ending on a WS row.

Shoulder shaping

Cast off 13 (14:15) sts at beg of next row.

Work 1 row straight, then cast off rem 13 (14:14) sts.

With RS facing, slip the center

20 (22:24) sts to a stitch holder. Rejoin yarn and patt to end of row. Dec 1 st at neck edge on the next 5 (5:7) rows, then on every foll alt row until 26 (28:29) sts rem.

Cont without shaping to match first side, ending on a RS row for shoulder shaping.

NEXT ROW (WS): Cast off 13 (14:15) sts, work 1 row straight, then cast off rem 13 (14:14) sts.

Sleeves

Using needles A and yarn B, cast on 45 (48:51) sts. Work rib as written for the back until the rib measures 2½in (6cm) from beg, ending on a RS row.

NEXT ROW: Inc row. [rib 2, M1] x 3, keeping rib correct, work across 33 (38:39) sts, [M1, rib 2] x 2(1:2), M1, rib 2. (51 (53:57) sts)

Change to needles B and work in patt as foll:

ROW 1 (RS): K12 (13:15) sts, p2, k8, p7, k8, p2, k12 (13:15) sts.

ROW 2 AND EVERY FOLL WS ROW: P12 (13:15) sts, k2, p8, k7, p8, k2, p12 (13:15) sts.

This sets the position for the central patt. **Cont working cable and bobble patt as for the back.**

At the same time, inc 1 st using your preferred increase (see pp.198–209) at each end of the 5th and every foll 6th row, until there are 85 (89:93) sts, working the new sts into the st st sides.

Cont without shaping until the sleeve measures 17½(17¾:18)in (44(45:46) cm) from beg ending on a WS row.

Shape sleeve head

Keeping patt as set, cast off 7 (7:8) sts at beg of next 2 rows. (71 (75:77) sts)

NEXT ROW: K1, skpo, patt to last 3sts, k2tog, k1.

NEXT ROW: P1, p2tog, patt to last 3sts, p2tog tbl, p1.

Rep last 2 rows 3 (3:4) times, then first row again. (57 (61:59) sts)

Then dec on every foll alt row until 27 (27:25) sts rem.

Dec on every row until 17 (19:21) sts rem. Cast off rem sts.

Neck band

Using needle C and yarn A, with RS facing, starting at left shoulder, pick up (see p.228) and k22 (23:22) sts down the front neck, k across 20(22:24) sts from front neck holder, pick up and k21 (22:22) sts up to shoulder seam, pick up and k 2sts down back neck, k across 38 (40:42) sts from back neck holder, pick up and k2 to shoulder. (105 (111:114) sts)

ROUND 1: K1, *p1, k2; rep from * to last 2sts, p1, k1.

Rep round 1 until you have completed 8 rounds.

Next round: Change to yarn B and k 2 rounds. Cast off loosely.

Finishing

Sew in all loose ends of yarn. Block pieces (see p.238) according to instructions on ballband. Join side and sleeve seams. Set in sleeve, matching the center of the sleeve to the shoulder seam and the underarm seam to the side seam.

Partial Fair Isle sweater

A generously loose-fitting sweater with Fair Isle bands, this knit is a good project for practicing Fair Isle colorwork technique (see p.215). There are no complicated shapings either, so you're free to focus on following the color changes and motifs instead.

✳ you will need

DIFFICULTY Moderate

SIZE To fit an adult woman, S (M:L)

YARN
Patons Classic Wool DK 50g

A x 12 (13:14)   **B** x 2 (2:2)

C x 3 (3:4)   **D** x 1 (1:1)

NEEDLES
A: 1 pair of US4 (3.5mm) needles
B: 1 pair of US6 (4mm/UK8) needles
C: 20in (50cm) long US4 (3.5mm) circular needle

GAUGE
22sts and 28 rows over 4in (10cm) worked in st st on US6 (4mm/UK8) needles

NOTIONS
2 stitch holders
Darning needle

How to make

Back

Using needles A and yarn A, cast on 129 (145:161) sts.
ROW 1 (RS): K2, p1, *k3, p1; rep from * to last 2sts, k2.
ROW 2: P2, k1, * p3, k1; rep from * to last 2sts, p2.
Rep these 2 rows until the rib measures 3in (8cm) from beg, ending on a WS row.
Change to needles B.
Beg with a k row, work in st st until the work measures 14in (35cm) from cast on, ending on a WS row.
Starting at stitch 1 on row 1, work from chart 1, reading all odd number (RS) rows from right to left and all even number (WS) rows from left to right until you have completed all 9 rows.
Work 7 rows st st using yarn A.
Work from stitch 1 on row 1 of chart 2 until you have completed all 23 rows.
Cont working in yarn A until the work measures 25(25½:26½)in (63(65:67)cm) from beg, ending on a WS row.

Back neck shaping

K across 40 (45:52) sts, turn, leave rem sts on a spare needle and work each side separately.
DEC ROW (WS): P1, p2tog, p to end of row.
ROW 2: K to last 3sts, k2tog, k1.
ROW 3: Rep row 1.
Cast off rem 37 (42:49) sts.
With RS facing, slip center 49 (55:57) sts to a holder. Rejoin yarn and knit to end of row.
ROW 1 (WS): P to last 3sts, p2tog tbl, p1.
ROW 2: K1, skpo, k to end of row.
ROW 3: Rep row 1.
Cast off rem 37 (42:49) sts.

Front

Work as for the back until the work measures 20¾ (21:22)in (53 (54:56)cm) from beg, ending on a WS row.

Front neck shaping

K across 55 (61:66) sts, turn, leave rem sts on a spare needle and work each side separately.

➤ This sweater is knitted in Patons Classic Wool DK Superwash in A: Red, B: Denim Heather, C: Aran, and D: Navy.

DEC ROW (WS): Cast off 3sts, p to end.

ROW 2: K to last 3sts, k2tog, k1. Rep rows 1–2 once more.

ROW 5: P1, p2tog, p to end of row.

ROW 6: Rep row 2. Rep rows 5–6 once more.

Then dec as set on every foll alt row until 37 (42:49) sts rem.

Cont without shaping until the front matches to the back shoulder, ending on a WS row. Cast off.

With RS facing, slip center 19 (23:29) sts to a holder for the front neck. Rejoin yarn and k to end of row.

DEC ROW (WS): P to last 3sts, p2tog tbl, p1.

ROW 2: Cast off 3sts, then k to end of row. Rep rows 1–2 once more.

ROW 5: Rep row 1.

ROW 6: K1, skpo, k to end of row. Rep rows 5–6 once more.

ROW 7: Rep row 1.

Dec as set on every foll alt row until 37 (42:49) sts rem.

Cont to match first side.

Sleeves

Using needles A and yarn A, cast on 49 (53:57) sts.

Work rib as written for the back until the rib measures 2½in (6cm) from beg, ending on a WS row.

Change to needles B.

Beg with a k row, work in st st throughout.

At the same time, inc 1 st (using your preferred increase (see pp.198–209) at each end of the 5th and every foll 6th row until there are 75(81:87) sts.

Work 3 (1:3) rows straight.

Work from chart 1, starting the pattern on 4th (1st:14th) st on row 1 of chart 1, and finishing on the 14th (1st:4th) st.

This sets the position for the patt.

Cont working as set from row 2 of chart 1 until all 9 rows have been worked. At the same time, cont to work side increases as set until there are 81 (85:93) sts.

When all 9 rows of chart 1 have been worked, work 7 rows using yarn A.

Work from chart 2, starting from 9th (15th:11th) st on row 1 of chart 2, and ending with 9th (3rd:7th) st.

All sizes

Cont until you have worked row 20 of chart 2.

Cast off loosely using yarn C.

Neckband

Join shoulder seams.

With RS facing, using yarn A and needle C, starting at the left shoulder, pick up and k26 (29:29) sts down to front neck, k across 19 (23:29) sts from front neck stitch holder, pick up and k26 (28:29) sts to shoulder seam, pick up and k 3sts down to back neck, k across 49 (55:57) sts from back neck stitch holder, pick up and k3 to shoulder seam. (126 (141:150) sts) Work 15 rounds of k2, p1 rib. Cast off loosely in rib.

Finishing

Sew in all loose ends. Block work according to instructions on ballband (see p.163 and p.238).

Pin the center of the sleeve to the shoulder seam and place a marker on the front and back to mark each end of the sleeve head, making sure marks are equal distance from the shoulder seam. Sew the sleeve head in place. Join side and sleeve seams.

Fair Isle bands up close Here you can see in detail the colorful motifs used on the sleeves and the body of this Fair Isle sweater.

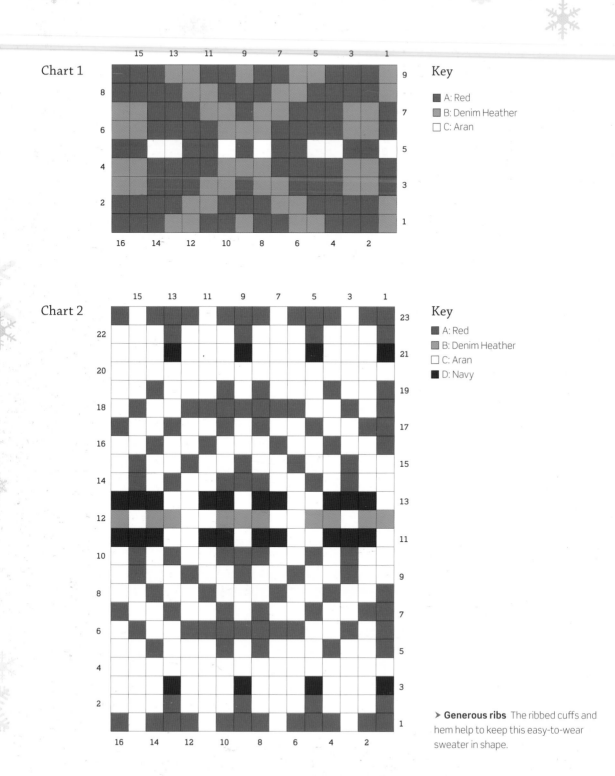

Chart 1

Chart 2

Key

A: Red
B: Denim Heather
C: Aran
D: Navy

> **Generous ribs** The ribbed cuffs and hem help to keep this easy-to-wear sweater in shape.

Cabled bobble hat

Knitting on big needles creates an impactful and cozy hat in no time, especially when combined with this super-chunky wool yarn. You'll need to use a large cable needle here to be able to hold the stitches securely when doing the cabling.

✻ you will need

DIFFICULTY Easy/moderate

SIZE To fit an adult woman

YARN
Rowan Big Wool 100g

A x 2

NEEDLES
1 pair of US15 (10mm/UK000) needles
Cable needle

GAUGE
9sts and 13 rows over 4in (10cm) in st st

NOTIONS
Darning needle

SPECIAL ABBREVIATIONS
C4F (Cross 2 front): Slip next 2sts to cable needle (cn) and hold at front of work, k2 from LH needle then k2 from cn.
C4B (Cross 4 back): Slip 2sts to cable needle (cn) and hold at back of work, k2 from LH needle then k2 from cn.

How to make

Brim
Cast on 48sts.
ROW 1: K1, [p2, k2] x 11, p2, k1.
ROW 2: P1, k2, [p2, k2] x 11, p1.
ROW 3: Rep row 1.
ROW 4: Rep row 2.
ROW 5: Rep row 1.
ROW 6: [K3, p6, k3] x 4.
ROW 7: [P3, C4F, k2, p3] x 4.
ROW 8 AND EVERY FOLL ALT ROW UNLESS OTHERWISE SPECIFIED: As row 6.
ROW 9: [P3, k2, C4B, p3] x 4.
ROWS 10–25: Rep rows 6–9 four times.
ROW 27: P2tog, p1, [C4F, k2, p2, s1, p2tog, psso, p1] x 3, C4F, k2, p1, p2tog. (40sts)
ROW 28: K2tog, [p6, s1, k2tog, psso, k1] x 3, p6, k2tog. (32sts)
ROW 29: K2tog, k1, s2 to cn, hold in back, k2, k2tog from cn, [p2tog, k2, s2 to cn, hold in back, k2, k2tog from cn] x 3, p1. (24sts)
ROW 30: [S1, p2tog, psso, p3] x 4. (16sts)
ROW 31: [S1, k2tog, psso, k1] x 4. (8sts)
ROW 32: [S1, p2tog, psso] x 2, p2tog. (3sts)
ROW 33: K3tog and pull long yarn tail through to secure.

Chunky cables The Rowan Big Wool yarn enhances the braided cable on this hat to great effect.

Finishing
Sew in all yarn ends and use the long yarn tail to sew the hat together using mattress stitch (see p.239). Use one ball of the yarn to make a pom-pom (see p.244) and then sew on the top.

➤ This hat is knitted in Rowan Big Wool in 061 Concrete.

top tip

Choose a contrasting color for the pom-pom and make your hat stand out from the crowd.

Slouchy hat

This luxurious-feeling hat is worked in a combination of flat and circular knitting. The cabled band is picked up on double-pointed needles; then, you create volume for the crown using increases and decreases. The silk–merino yarn gives it a delicious sheen and allows a soft drape.

❋ you will need

DIFFICULTY Moderate

SIZE To fit an adult woman

YARN Fyberspates
Scrumptious Chunky 100g

A x 2

NEEDLES
A: 1 pair of US10 (6mm/UK4)
needles
B: 4 x US10 (6mm/UK4)
double-pointed needles
C: Cable needle

GAUGE
18sts x 20 rows over 4in
(10cm) in reverse st st

NOTIONS
Darning needle

SPECIAL ABBREVIATIONS
C4B: Slip next 2sts to cable
needle (cn) and hold at back of
work, k next 2sts from LH
needle then k 2sts from cn.
C4F: Slip next 2sts to cn and
hold at front of work, k next
2sts from LH needle then
k 2sts from cn.

How to make

Brim
Using needles A, cast on 20sts.
ROW 1: K.
ROW 2 AND EVERY FOLL ALT ROW: K2,
p to last 2sts, k2.
ROW 3: K.
ROW 5: K2, *C4B; rep from * to last
2sts, k2.
ROW 7: K.
ROW 9: K.
ROW 11: K4, *C4F; rep from * to last
4sts, k4.
ROW 12: K2, p to last 2sts, k2.
Rep rows 1–12, until brim measures
20in (50cm), ending on row 12.
Cast off. Join cast-on edge to
cast-off edge.

Crown
Using needles B, with RS facing and
beg at back seam, pick up and k96
along top edge of brim.
P 1 round.
ROUND 1–5: P.
ROUND 6: *Kfb; rep from * to end of
round. (192sts)
ROUNDS 7–11: K.
ROUND 12: *K2tog; rep from * to end
of round. (96sts)
Rep rounds 1–12 twice more.

NEXT ROUND: *P10, p2tog; rep from *
to end of round. (88sts)
NEXT ROUND: P.
NEXT ROUND: *P9, p2tog; rep from * to
end of round. (80sts)
NEXT ROUND: P.
NEXT ROUND: *P8, p2tog; rep from * to
end of round. (72sts)
NEXT ROUND: *P7, p2tog; rep from * to
end of round. (64sts)
NEXT ROUND: *P6, p2tog; rep from * to
end of round. (56sts)
NEXT ROUND: *P5, p2tog; rep from * to
end of round. (48sts)
NEXT ROUND: *P4, p2tog; rep from * to
end of round. (40sts)
NEXT ROUND: *P3, p2tog; rep from * to
end of round. (32sts)
NEXT ROUND: *P2, p2tog; rep from * to
end of round. (24sts)
NEXT ROUND: *P1, p2tog; rep from * to
end of round. (16sts)
NEXT ROUND: *P2tog; rep from * to end
of round. (8sts)
Break yarn, thread through stitches,
pull tightly, tie, and leave long tail.

Finishing
Weave in all yarn ends with a darning
needle.

◄ This hat uses Fyberspates
Scrumptious Chunky in 200 Cherry.

❄ you will need

DIFFICULTY Easy/moderate

SIZE To fit an adult woman

YARN
Rowan Felted Tweed Aran 50g

A x 1 **B** x 1

NEEDLES
1 pair of US8 (5mm/UK6)
needles
Cable needle

GAUGE
16sts and 23 rows over 4in
(10cm) in st st

SPECIAL ABBREVIATIONS
C8F (Cross 8 front): (on RS) slip
4sts to cable needle (cn), hold
in front, k4, then k4 from cn.
C8B (Cross 8 back): (on RS) slip
4sts to cn, hold in back, k4,
then k4 from cn.

Wrist warmers

The glorious braided cable pattern sings loud from these stylish wrist warmers, which allow your fingers freedom to do buttons and find keys. The two-stitch rib fits the glove snugly to the wrist, and the wonderful fleck adds extra interest to this tweedy wool yarn.

How to make

Left hand

Using yarn A, cast on 35sts.
ROW 1: P1, [k2, p2] x 4, p14, k2, p2.
ROW 2: K2, p2, k2, p12, [k2, p2] x 4, k1.
ROW 3: P1, [k2, p2] x 4, k12, p2, k2, p2.
ROW 4: As row 2.
ROW 5: P1, [k2, p2] x 4, C8F, k4, p2, k2, p2.
ROW 6: As row 2.
ROW 7: As row 3.
ROW 8: As row 2.
ROW 9: P1, [k2, p2] x 4, k4, C8B, p2, k2, p2.
ROW 10: As row 2.
ROW 11: As row 3.
ROW 12: As row 2.
ROW 13: As row 5.
ROW 14: As row 2.
ROW 15: As row 3.
Change to yarn B.
ROW 16 AND EVERY FOLL ALT ROW: P.
ROW 17: [K1, p1] x 8, k5, C8B, [k1, p1] x 3.
ROW 19: [P1, k1] x 8, p1, k12, [p1, k1] x 3.

◀ These wrist warmers use Rowan Felted Tweed Aran in A: 729 Soot and B: 731 Plum.

ROW 21: [k1, p1] x 8, k1, C8F, k4, [k1, p1] x 3.
ROW 23: As row 19.
ROWS 25–30: As rows 17–22.
ROW 31: [P1, k1] x 4, cast off 6sts, k1, p1, k12, [p1, k1] x 3.
ROW 32: P21, cast on 6sts, p8.
ROWS 33–40: As rows 17–24.
ROW 41: As row 9.
ROW 42: As row 2.
ROW 43: As row 3.
Change to yarn A.
ROW 44: As row 2.
ROW 45: As row 5.
ROW 46: As row 2.
Cast off tightly purlwise.

Right hand

Using yarn A, cast on 35sts.
ROW 1: P2, k2, p14, [p2, k2] x 4, p1.
ROW 2: K1, [p2, k2] x 4, p12, k2, p2, k2.
ROW 3: P2, k2, p2, k12, [p2, k2] x 4, p1.
ROW 4: As row 2.
ROW 5: P2, k2, p2, C8F, k4, [p2, k2] x 4, p1.
ROW 6: As row 2.
ROW 7: As row 3.
ROW 8: As row 2.
ROW 9: P2, k2, p2, k4, C8B, [p2, k2] x 4, p1.
ROW 10: As row 2.

ROW 11: As row 3.
ROW 12: As row 2.
ROW 13: As row 5.
ROW 14: As row 2.
ROW 15: As row 3.
Change to yarn B.
ROW 16 AND EVERY FOLL ALT ROW: P.
ROW 17: [P1, k1] x 3, k4, C8B, k1, [p1, k1] x 8.
ROW 19: [K1, p1] x 3, k12, p1, [k1, p1] x 8.
ROW 21: [P1, k1] x 3, C8F, k5, [p1, k1] x 8.
ROW 23: As row 19.
ROWS 25–30: As rows 17–22.
ROW 31: [K1, p1] x 3, k12, p1, k1, p1, cast off 6sts, p1, [k1, p1] x 3.
ROW 32: P8, cast on 6sts, p21.
ROWS 33–40: As rows 17–24.
ROW 41: As row 9.
ROW 42: As row 2.
ROW 43: As row 3.
Change to yarn A.
ROW 44: As row 2.
ROW 45: As row 5.
ROW 46: As row 2.
Cast off tightly purlwise.

Finishing

With wrong sides facing, sew up the side using a neat whipstitch (see p.240) and matching up the colors.

To make these
projects, from
left to right, see pages
104–105, 66–69,
124–125, 70–73

Ruched scarf

This scarf isn't your average scarf. For one thing, you knit it widthwise on a long, circular needle, and for another, it uses a wonderfully luxurious mix of yarns—merino, alpaca, and silk—so is beautifully soft and drapey, allowing the pattern's ruching to take center stage.

❄ you will need

DIFFICULTY Moderate

SIZE 6 x 45in (15 x 115cm)

YARN
Mirasol Sulka 50g

A x 4

NEEDLES
A: 40in (100cm) long US9 (5.5mm/UK5) circular needle
B: 40in (100cm) long US10½ (6.5mm/UK3) circular needle

GAUGE
18sts and 19 rows over 4in (10cm) in st st on 6.5mm US10½ (6.5mm/UK3) needles

How to make

With needle B, loosely cast on 121sts. The cast-on and cast-off rows are very visible, so use cable cast-on (see p180) to match the chain cast-off.
Change to needle A.
ROW 1 (WS): P.
**ROWS 2-3: K.
ROW 4: K2, *yo, k2tog; rep from * to last st, k1.
ROWS 5-6: K.
ROW 7: P.
Change to needle B.
ROW 8: Kfb to end. (242sts)
ROW 9: P.
ROW 10: K.
Rep rows 9 and 10 three more times.
Change to needle A.
NEXT ROW: P2tog to end. (121sts)
Rep from ** once more, then rep rows 2–6.
Change to needle B.
Cast off loosely purlwise.

Finishing
Lightly block (see p.238) to size.

Novel use of increases This scarf uses a combination of yarn-overs (increases) and decreases to create the lace holes running end to end. These increases and decreases create the ruching.

◄ This scarf is knitted in Mirasol Sulka in 200 Snow White.

Short cabled socks

These soft and cozy ankle-length bed or slipper socks are knitted flat, not in the round. They have a textured chevron cable pattern to the top and back; the sole is worked in reverse stockinette stitch. As with all cables, once you have the pattern's rhythm the knitting grows fast.

❄ you will need

DIFFICULTY Moderate/Difficult

SIZE To fit an adult woman, shoe size US 6½–8½

YARN
Debbie Bliss Baby Cashmerino 50g

A x 2

NEEDLES
1 pair of US3 (3.25mm/UK10) needles
Cable needle

GAUGE
26sts x 30 rows over 4in (10cm) in st st

SPECIAL ABBREVIATIONS
C4F: Slip 2sts to cable needle (cn) and hold in front, k2, then k2 from cn.

C4B: Slip 2sts to cn and hold in back, k2, then k2 from cn.

C8F: Slip 4sts to cn and hold in front, k4, then k4 from cn.

C8B: Slip 4sts to cn and hold in back, k4, then k4 from cn.

◄ These socks are made with Debbie Bliss Baby Cashmerino in 71.

How to make

Right foot
Cast on 57sts.
ROW 1: K1, [p2, k2] x 14.
ROW 2: [P2, k2] x 14, p1.
ROWS 3-12: Rep rows 1-2.
ROW 13: K.
ROW 14 AND EVERY FOLL ALT ROW UNLESS SPECIFIED OTHERWISE: P.
ROW 15: K29, C4F, k1, C8F, C8B, k1, C4B, k2.
ROW 17: K10, C4F, C4B, k39.
ROW 19: K29, C4F, k18, C4B, k2.
ROW 21: Rep row 17.
ROWS 23-33: Rep rows 15-22, then rep rows 15-17.
ROW 34: P56, turn.

The heel
S1, k24, turn work. Leave rem sts on a stitch holder for instep. **
S1, p22, turn work.
S1, k20, turn work.
S1, p18, turn work.
S1, k16, turn work.
S1, p14, turn work.
S1, k12, turn work.
S1, p10, turn work.
S1, k8, turn work.
S1, p6, s1, turn work.

In the next instructions you'll be adding back in the unworked stitches from the heel. When you are working these, make sure they are not twisted.
K8, s1, turn work.
P10, s1, turn work.
K12, s1, turn work.
P14, s1, turn work.
K16, s1, turn work.
P18, s1, turn work.
K20, s1, turn work.
P22, s2sts, turn work.
K24, s1, turn work.**
P26.

Instep and sole
ROW 35: K2, p24, k3, C4F, k18, C4B, k2.
ROW 36 AND EVERY FOLL ALT ROW UNLESS SPECIFIED OTHERWISE: P31, k24, p2.
ROW 37: K2, p24, k31.
ROW 39: K2, p24, k3, C4F, k1, C8F, C8B, k1, C4B, k2.
ROW 41: Rep row 37.
ROWS 43-74: Rep rows 35-42 four times.
ROW 75: Rep row 35.
ROW 76: P.
ROW 77 AND EVERY FOLL ALT ROW: K.
ROWS 78-79: Rep rows 76-77.

Shaping the toe

ROW 80: P2tog, p25, s1, p2tog, psso, p25, p2tog.

ROW 82: P2tog, p23, s1, p2tog, psso, p23, p2tog.

ROW 84: P2tog, p21, s1, p2tog, psso, p21, p2tog.

ROW 86: P2tog, p19, s1, p2tog, psso, p19, p2tog.

ROW 88: P2tog, p17, s1, p2tog, psso, p17, p2tog.

ROW 90: P2tog, p15, s1, p2tog, psso, p15, p2tog.

ROW 92: P2tog, p13, s1, p2tog, psso, p13, p2tog.

ROW 93: Cast off and leave long tail.

Left foot

Cast on 57sts.

ROW 1: [K2, p2] x 14, k1.

ROW 2: P1, [k2, p2] x 14.

ROWS 3-12: Rep rows 1-2.

ROW 13: K.

ROW 14 AND EVERY FOLL ALT ROW UNLESS SPECIFIED OTHERWISE: P.

ROW 15: K2, C4F, k1, C8F, C8B, k1, C4B, k29.

ROW 17: K39, C4F, C4B, k10.

ROW 19: K2, C4F, k18, C4B, k29.

ROW 21: Rep row 17.

ROWS 23-33: Rep rows 15-22, then rep rows 15-17.

ROW 34: P27, turn. Leave rem sts on a stitch holder for instep.

The heel

S1, k24, turn work.

Work as for the heel of the right foot from ** to **.

P57.

Instep and sole

ROW 35: K2, C4F, k18, C4B, k3, p24, k2.

ROW 36 AND EVERY FOLL ALT ROW UNLESS SPECIFIED OTHERWISE: P2, k24, p31.

ROW 37: K31, p24, k2.

ROW 39: K2, C4F, k1, C8F, C8B, k1, C4B, k3, p24, k2.

ROW 41: Rep row 37.

ROWS 43-74: Rep rows 35-42 four times.

ROW 75: Rep row 35.

ROW 76: P.

ROW 77 AND EVERY FOLL ALT ROW UNLESS SPECIFIED OTHERWISE: K.

ROWS 78-79: Rep rows 76-77.

Shaping the toe

ROW 80: P2tog, p25, s1, p2tog, psso, p25, p2tog.

ROW 82: P2tog, p23, s1, p2tog, psso, p23, p2tog.

ROW 84: P2tog, p21, s1, p2tog, psso, p21, p2tog.

ROW 86: P2tog, p19, s1, p2tog, psso, p19, p2tog.

ROW 88: P2tog, p17, s1, p2tog, psso, p17, p2tog.

ROW 90: P2tog, p15, s1, p2tog, psso, p15, p2tog.

ROW 92: P2tog, p13, s1, p2tog, psso, p13, p2tog.

ROW 93: Cast off and leave a long tail.

Finishing

Pull through the long yarn tail, and with RS facing use it to graft the toe ends together. Sew the side seam with a neat whipstitch (see p.240), matching the rows together.

top tip

Take your time when
sewing up these socks so
the seams are smooth
and durable.

Boot cuffs

When the weather demands pulling on some boots, what could be better to bridge the gap between sock and boot, or just for an extra layer of warmth, than these boot cuffs? And they're not just for wearing with rain boots—fold over the top of leather boots and step out in style.

❄ you will need

DIFFICULTY Moderate

SIZE To fit an average 14in (36cm) calf, 6¾in (17cm) deep

YARN
Lana Grossa Alta Moda
Alpaca 100g

A x 2

NEEDLES
A: 4 x US6 (4mm/UK8) double-pointed needles or a short circular needle
B: 4 x US8 (5mm/UK6) double-pointed needles or a short circular needle
C: Cable needle

GAUGE
20sts and 25 rows over 4in (10cm) in cable patt on US8 (5mm/UK6) needles

NOTIONS
Darning needle
Stitch marker

SPECIAL ABBREVIATIONS
C8B: (on RS) Slip 4sts to cable needle (cn), hold in back, k4, k4 from cn.
C8F: (on RS) Slip 4sts to cn, hold in front, k4, k4 from cn.

How to make

Boot cuffs (make 2)
With needles B, cast on 72sts.
Join in the round (see p.224), being careful not to twist sts. Place st marker at start of round. The boot cuff is worked from bottom to top.
ROUND 1: *K1, [p2, k2] x 3, p2, k1, p2; rep from * to end.
Rep this round 8 more times.
CABLE ROUND: *C8B, C8F, p2; rep from * to end.
These 10 rounds form the repeat.
Work the repeat 2 more times.
Rep round 1 four times.
NEXT ROUND: P to end.
Change to needles A.
NEXT ROUND: *K1, p1; rep from * to end of row.
Rep this last round 7 more times.

Picot cast-off
Cast off 2sts in rib st patt.
*Pass the rem st to the LH needle.
Cast on 2sts.
Cast off 6sts in rib st patt.
Rep from * ending last rep with cast-off 4sts.

Cables up close Here you can see the "wishbone" cables along with the delicate picot edging at the top.

Finishing
Weave in all yarn ends with a darning needle and block (see p.238) to finish.

◄ These cuffs are knitted in Lana Grossa Alta Moda Alpaca in 8 Teal.

Projects for Men

Textured sweater

The interesting texture in this chunky sweater has been created by using a simple all-over cable pattern on the wrong side of the knitting. The honeycomb stitch ensures that this will be an incredibly warm sweater, as well as a comfy one, since there is lots of stretch in this stitch.

❄ you will need

DIFFICULTY Moderate

SIZE To fit an adult man S (M:L)

YARN Rowan Felted Tweed DK 50g

A x 10 (11:12)

NEEDLES
A: 1 pair of US6 (4mm/UK8) needles
B: 1 pair of US7 (4.5mm/UK7) needles
C: Cable needle
D: 32in (80cm) long US6 (4mm/UK8) circular needle

GAUGE
24sts and 26 rows over 4in (10cm) in cable patt on US7 (4.5mm/UK7) needles

NOTIONS
Darning needle
2 stitch holders or spare needles

SPECIAL ABBREVIATIONS
T3F (Twist 3 front): Slip next 2sts to cable needle (cn) and hold at front of work, p2, then k1 from cn.
T3B (Twist 3 back): Slip next 2sts to cn and hold at back of work, k1, p2 from cn.

How to make

Details of actual measurements:
Chest 40–42(44-46:48-50)in (102-107(112-117:122-127)cm)
Length to back neck 27(27½:28)in (69(70:71)cm)
Sleeve seam 21(21½:22)in (53(54:55)cm)
Please note that the cable pattern is on the wrong side of this work.

Back

Using needles A, cast on 134 (140:146) sts.
ROW 1 (RS): P2, *k4, p2; rep from * to end.
ROW 2: K2, *p4, k2; rep from * to end.
Rep these 2 rows until the work measures 4in (10cm) from beg ending on a RS row.
Change to needles B, and cont in patt as foll:
ROW 1 (WS): K1, *T3F, T3B; rep from * to last st, k1.
ROW 2: K3, p2, *k4, p2; rep from * to last 3sts, k3.

ROW 3: P3, k2, *p4, k2; rep from * to last 3sts, p3.
ROW 4: As row 2.
ROW 5: K1, *T3B, T3F; rep from * to last st, k1.
ROW 6: P2, *k4, p2; rep from * to end.
ROW 7: K2, *p4, k2; rep from * to end.
ROW 8: Rep row 6.
Rep these 8 rows until the work measures 17(17½:18)in (43(44:45)cm) from cast-on edge, ending on a WS row.

Shape armholes

Keeping patt correct throughout, cast off 6 (7:8) sts at beg of next 2 rows. (122 (126:130) sts)
Dec 1 st at each end of the next 7 rows. (108 (112:116) sts)
Then on foll 5 (4:3) alt rows. (98 (104:110) sts)
Cont without shaping until the armhole measures 9(9¼:9½)in (22(23:24)cm) from beg of shaping, ending on a WS row.

◄ This sweater is made using Rowan Felted Tweed DK in 173 Duck Egg.

Shape shoulders and back neck

Cast off 9 (10:11) sts at beg of next 2 rows. (80 (84:88) sts)

NEXT ROW (RS): Cast off 9 (10:11) sts, patt until 11sts rem on right needle and turn, leaving rem sts on a holder. Work each side of neck separately.

Cast off 3sts at beg of next row, patt to end of row.

Cast off rem 8sts.

With RS facing, slip center 40 (42:44) sts to holder for back neck, rejoin yarn, and patt to end of row.

NEXT ROW (WS): Cast off 9 (10:11) sts, patt to end of row.

Cast off 3sts at beg of next row, patt to end of row.

Cast off rem 8sts.

Front

Work as for the back until the armhole measures 4(4¼:5)in (10(11:12)cm) from beg of shaping, ending on a WS row.

Front neck shaping

Keeping patt correct throughout, patt across 39 (41:43) sts, turn, leave rem sts on a holder. Work each side of neck separately.

Dec 1 st at the neck edge on the next 7 rows. (32 (34:36) sts)

Then dec on every foll alt row until 26 (28:30) sts rem.

Cont without shaping until the front matches the back to the shoulders, ending on a WS row.

Shape shoulders

Cast off 9 (10:11) sts at beg of next 2 RS rows.

Work 1 row straight, then cast off rem 8sts.

With RS facing, slip center 20 (22:24) sts to a holder for the front neck. Rejoin yarn and patt to end of row.

Dec 1 st at neck edge on the next 7 rows, then on every foll alt row until 26 (28:30) sts rem. Cont to match first side ending on a RS row.

Shape shoulders

Cast off 9 (10:11) sts at beg of next 2 WS rows. Work 1 row straight, then cast off rem 8sts.

Sleeves

Using needles A, cast on 50 (56:56) sts. Work rib as written for the back until the rib measures 3in (8cm) from beg ending on a RS row.

Change to needles B, and work in patt as for back.

At the same time, inc 1 st at each end of 5th and every foll 4th row until there are 74 (76:76) sts, then on every foll 6th row until there are 90 (92:96) sts, working the new sts into the patt.

Cont without shaping until the sleeve measures 20(20:20½)in (50(51:52)cm) from beg, ending on a WS row.

Shape sleeve head

Cast off 6 (7:8) sts at beg of next 2 rows. (78 (78:80) sts)

Dec 1 st at each end of the next 7 rows. (64 (64:66) sts)

Then dec 1 st at each end of the next 4 (6:4) foll alt rows. (56 (52:58) sts)

Dec 1 st at each end of next 4 (2:2)

foll 4th rows. (48 (48:54) sts)

Dec 1 st at each end of every foll alt row to 24 (22:38) sts, then dec 1 st at each end on every row to 18 (26:28) sts.

1st size only

Cast off rem 18 sts.

2nd & 3rd sizes only

Cast off 4sts at beg of next 2 rows. (18:20sts)

Cast off.

Neckband

Join the shoulder seams matching the pattern.

With RS facing using needle D, and starting at the left shoulder, pick up and k25 (26:28) sts down to front neck, k across 20 (22:24) sts from front neck holder, pick up and k25 (26:28) sts to shoulder, pick up and k 5sts to back neck, k across 40 (42:44) sts from back neck holder, pick up and k 5sts to shoulder seam. Join to work in the round. (120 (126:134) sts)

ROUND 1: K4 (4:0), p2, *k4, p2; rep from * to end.

Work in rib as set for another 8 rounds, then cast off in rib.

Finishing

Join side and sleeve seams being careful to match pattern. Set in sleeve matching the center of the sleeve to the shoulder seam and the underarm seam to the side seam. Sew in all yarn ends and block (see p.238) according to ballband instructions.

DIFFICULTY Moderate

SIZE To fit an adult man, foot length 10in (25cm) (adjustable)

YARN
Rowan Felted Tweed DK 50g

A x 2

NEEDLES
A: 1 pair of US3 (3.25mm/UK10) needles
B: 1 pair of US5 (3.75mm/UK9) needles
Spare needle

GAUGE
24sts and 32 rows over 4in (10cm) in st st on US5 (3.75mm/UK9) needles

NOTIONS
Stitch holder
Darning needle

Ribbed socks

These roomy socks are knitted flat, not in the round. The chunky rib gives them a rough-and-ready texture, but the sole is a smoother stockinette stitch. To ensure your socks fit perfectly, measure the length of the foot before you start, so you can adjust the length as necessary.

How to make

Socks (make 2)
With needles A, cast on 62sts.
Work in 2 x 2 rib as foll:
ROW 1 (RS): K2, *p2, k2; rep from * to end.
ROW 2: P2, *k2, p2; rep from * to end.
Work in rib for another 8 rows.
Change to needles B and cont in rib as set until work measures 9½in (24cm) from cast-on edge, ending with row 2.

Divide for heel
Break off yarn. With RS facing, slip first 16sts onto RH needle, place center 30sts onto holder for instep, slip last 16sts onto spare needle. With WS facing, rejoin yarn to first 16sts, *k2, p2, rep from * to last 4sts, k2, p2tog. Cont row working across sts on spare needle as foll: p2tog, k2, p2 to last 2sts, k2. (30sts) Change to needles A and work as foll:
ROW 1 (RS): P2, *k2, p2; rep from * to end.
ROW 2: K2, *p2, k2; rep from * to end.
Rep these 2 rows 9 times more.

Turn heel
Work in st st as foll:
ROW 1: K16, skpo, k1, turn.
ROW 2: P4, p2tog, p1, turn.
ROW 3: K5, skpo, k1, turn.
ROW 4: P6, p2tog, p1, turn.
ROW 5: K7, skpo, k1, turn.
ROW 6: P8, p2tog, p1, turn.
Cont to dec as set until 11 rows have been worked.
ROW 12: P14, p2tog, p1, turn.
ROW 13: K to end.
ROW 14: P to end. (18sts)
Break off yarn.
With RS facing, rejoin yarn to instep and pick up 12sts evenly along the side edge of the heel, k across 18sts of heel, pick up and k12 evenly along the other side of the heel. (42sts)
NEXT ROW: P.
ROW 1: K1, skpo, k to last 3sts, k2tog, k1.
ROWS 2 AND 4: P.
ROW 3: K.
Rep these 4 rows 4 times more, then rows 1 and 2 once more. (30sts) Change to needles B and continue in st st until work measures 9in (22cm) from back of heel, ending with a WS row. (Length of foot can be adjusted here.)

Shape toe
ROW 1: *K1, skpo, k to last 3sts, k2tog, k1.
ROW 2: P1, p2tog, p to last 3sts, p2tog tbl, p1.
Rep these last 2 rows three times more. (14sts)*
Leave these sts on a spare needle.

Instep
With RS facing and needles B, rejoin yarn to 30sts on stitch holder and work in k2, p2 rib as before, until foot measures 9in (22cm), ending with a WS row. Shape toe from * to * as for lower foot.
With RS sides facing, cast off as foll: p tog 1 st from each needle and cast off as each st is worked.

Finishing
Join the upper to lower foot and sew together at both sides. Join the back ankle seam.

◄ These socks are made with Rowan Felted Tweed DK in 170 Seafarer.

To make these
projects, from left to
right, see pages
106–109, 32–35,
118–119

✳

top tip

This acrylic yarn wears
well, but a wool yarn would
be more luxurious and
work well, too.

Beanie hat

The interesting combination of knit and purl stitches adds texture to this close-fitting beanie, and the yarn used here shows the pattern off to full effect. You'll be able to knit this hat up fast, too, since it's worked in a chunky-weight yarn.

❄ you will need

DIFFICULTY Easy

SIZE To fit an adult man

YARN
Berroco Comfort
Chunky 100g

A x 1

NEEDLES
1 pair of US10½
(6.5mm/UK3) needles

GAUGE
14sts and 20 rows over
4in (10cm) in st st

NOTIONS
Darning needle

How to make

Brim
Cast on 54sts.
ROW 1: [K2, p2] x 13, k2.
ROW 2: P2, [k2, p2] x 13.
ROWS 3-6: Rep rows 1-2.
ROW 7: Rep row 1.

Crown
ROW 8: K2, [k2, p2, k4] x 6, k2, p2.
ROW 9: [K2, p6] x 6, k2, p4.
ROW 10: P4, k2, [p6, k2] x 6.
ROW 11: [P2, k6] x 6, p2, k4.
ROWS 12-13: As rows 10-11.
ROWS 14-25: Rep rows 8-13.
ROWS 26-27: Rep rows 8-9.
ROWS 28-35: Rep rows 10-11.
ROW 36: [P2tog, p2, k2, p2] x 6, p2tog, p2, k2. (47sts)
ROW 37: [P2, k1, k2tog, k2] x 6, p2, k1, k2tog. (40sts)
ROW 38: P2, [k2tog, p1, p2tog, p1] x 6, k2tog. (27sts)
ROW 39: [P1, s1, k2tog, psso] x 6, p1, k2tog. (14sts)
ROW 40: [S1, p2tog, psso] x 4, p2tog. (5sts)

ROW 41: K all 5sts together and pull long piece of yarn through.

Finishing
Use the long piece of yarn and darning needle to sew up the seam using mattress stitch (see p.239).

◄ This beanie uses
Berroco Comfort
Chunky in 5713 Dusk.

Cabled scarf

This textured scarf doesn't at first glance look like a classic cable knit. The four-needle cable is worked on alternating rows, so what you get is a dense, woven-looking piece. The choice of merino and kid mohair yarn emphasizes the textural quality of this super-cozy knit.

❄ you will need

DIFFICULTY Moderate

SIZE To fit an adult man

YARN
Rowan Cocoon 100g

A x 5

NEEDLES
1 pair of US10½
(7mm/UK2) needles
Cable needle

GAUGE
26sts and 20 rows over 4in
(10cm) in cable patt

SPECIAL ABBREVIATIONS
C4F (cross 4 front): Sl next
2sts to cable needle (cn) and
hold at front of work, k next
2sts from LH needle, then
k 2sts from cn.
C4B (cross 4 back): Sl next
2sts to cn and hold at back
of work, k next 2sts from LH
needle, then k 2sts from cn.

How to make

Cast on 64sts.
ROW 1: *K1, p1, rep from * to end
of row.
ROW 2: *P1, k1, rep from * to end
of row.
ROW 3: *C4F, rep from * to end of row.
ROW 4: P.
ROW 5: K2, *C4B, rep from * to last
2 sts, k2.
ROW 6: P.
Rep rows 3–6 until the scarf measures
59in (150cm), or desired length,
ending with row 6.
Rep rows 1–2.
Cast off.

Finishing
Weave in all ends with darning needle
and block (see p.238).

➤ This scarf uses Rowan
Cocoon in 816 Kiwi.

Slouchy hat

This roomy hat is essentially a supersized rib knitted in the round with a soft, rolling rim, knitted here in red. Personalize the hat with the combinations you choose for the main and accent colors. The incredibly soft and warm merino yarn is sure to make it a big hit.

❄ you will need

DIFFICULTY Moderate

SIZE To fit an average adult man (actual measurement around roll 22in/55cm)

YARN
Debbie Bliss Rialto Aran 50g (100% wool)

A x 1   **B** x 2

NEEDLES
A: 4 x US6 (4mm/UK8) double-pointed needles
B: 4 x US6 (4mm/UK8) double-pointed needles

GAUGE
18sts and 24 rows over 4in (10cm) in st st on US8 (5mm/UK6) needles

NOTIONS
Stitch marker
Darning needle

How to make

Roll of hat
Using needles A and yarn A, cast on 110sts. Join in the round (see p.224), being careful not to twist sts. Place st marker to indicate start of round.
Work 7 rounds in st st (k every st on every round).

Band of hat
Change to yarn B.
ROUND 1: K to end.
Work 12 rounds in 1 x 1 rib (*k1, p1; rep from * to end).

Body of hat
Change to needles B.
INC ROUND: [K11, M1] to end. (120sts)
ROUND 1: [P5, k5] to end.
ROUND 2: K to end.
Rep rounds 1 and 2 until work measures 10in (25cm) from rolled edge, finishing with round 1.

Shape crown
ROUND 1: K2, *k2tog, k3; rep from * to last 3sts, k2tog, k1. (96sts)
ROUND 2: [P4, k4] to end.
ROUND 3: K1, *k2tog, k2; rep from * to last 3sts, k2tog, k1. (72sts)
ROUND 4: [P3, k3] to end.
ROUND 5: [K1, k2tog] to end. (48sts)
ROUND 6: [P2, k2] to end.
ROUND 7: K2tog to end. (24sts)
ROUND 8: K2tog to end. (12sts)
Break yarn, thread through rem sts, and tighten to close.

Finishing
Weave in yarn ends using a darning needle. Lightly block (see p.239) the body of the hat, but not the rib.

◄ This hat is knitted in Debbie Bliss Rialto Aran in A: 18 Red and B: 29 Mid Grey.

Projects for
Home

Chunky cable lap blanket

Who could resist snuggling under this chunky merino wool blanket when it's cold outside? The snaking cables that wind their way across the blanket are emphasized by the textural strips of garter stitch between them.

❋ you will need

DIFFICULTY Moderate

SIZE 37 x 49in (95 x 125cm)

YARN
Rowan Big Wool 100g

A x 9

NEEDLES
1 pair of US19 (15mm)
needles or 1 x 40in (100cm)
circular needle
Cable needle

GAUGE
7sts and 13 rows over 4in
(10cm) in g st

NOTIONS
Darning needle

SPECIAL ABBREVIATIONS
C6F (Cable 6 Front): Slip 3sts to
cable needle (cn) and hold at
front of work, k3 from LH
needle then k3 from cn.
C6B (Cable 6 Back): Slip 3sts to
cn, hold at back of work, k3
then k3 from cn.

How to make

Lap blanket
Cast on 84sts. (As the cast-on and cast-off rows are visible, we have used cable cast on (see p.180) to match the chain cast-off).

Border
Working back and forth along the circular needle as if working even, work 6 rows in g st (k to end).

Cable design
ROWS 1 AND 3: K.
ROW 2 AND EVERY FOLL ALT ROW TILL
ROW12: K3, *p6, k3; rep from * to end.
ROW 5: K3, *C6F, k3; rep from * to end.
ROWS 7 AND 9: K.
ROW 11: K3, *C6B, k3; rep from * to end.
Rep rows 1–12 ten times.

Border
Work 6 rows of g st (K to end).
Cast off.

Finishing
Weave in all yarn ends and lightly steam (see Blocking, p.238) to the right size.

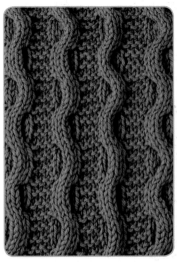

An attractive combination of snaking cables and interspersed panels of garter stitch make a chunky, cozy blanket that is a delight to knit.

◄ This lap blanket is knitted in Rowan Big Wool in 058 Heather.

Patchwork blanket

This blanket is in the simplest stitch—garter stitch—and can be as small or as large as you like. To mix things up a little, you can rotate alternate squares by 90° when sewing up the squares so that you create some texture within the blanket, or even choose some different stitch patterns, remembering to check the gauge and size of each square.

❄ you will need

DIFFICULTY Easy

SIZE Each square is 4in (10cm) square, so simply work out how big or small you want your blanket to be. This blanket for a single bed has 12 x 16 squares.

YARN
Any part-balls of aran-weight or DK yarn will work for this blanket. Adjust the gauge to suit your yarn specifications.

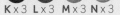

A x 3 B x 3 C x 3 D x 3 E x 3

F x 3 G x 3 H x 3 I x 3 J x 3

K x 3 L x 3 M x 3 N x 3

NEEDLES
A: 1 pair of US6 (4mm/UK8) needles
B: 48in (120cm) long US6 (4mm/UK8) circular needle (optional, for border only)

GAUGE
20sts and 40 rows over 4in (10cm) in g st

NOTIONS
Darning needle

How to make

The beauty of this pattern is that it allows you to use different weight yarns. However, if you find that some squares are knitting up too bulky, reduce the number of rows and stitches and/or increase the needle size for that type of yarn.

Finishing the squares
Using needles A, cast on 20sts.
K for 40 rows and cast off.
Rep to make desired number of squares.

Square by square This simple project is a great stash buster and one to turn to between more demanding knits.

◀ This blanket uses Debbie Bliss Rialto DK in A: 17 Navy, B: 34 Fuchsia, C: 45 Gold, D: 56 Tangerine, E: 44 Aqua, F: 60 Sky, G: 61 Plum, H: 50 Deep Rose, I: 49 Blush, J: 19 Duck Egg, K: 10 Moss, L: 53 Basil, M: 04 Grey, N: 66 Vintage Pink. You can make a more or less varied choice of colors depending on your preference.

Joining the squares

Using a neutral or matching color, carefully sew the squares together using either mattress stitch (see p.239) or by whipstitching (see p.240) along the side edges of the squares. Whipstitch along the tops and bottoms of the squares.

Adding the edge

If you'd like a border to bring the whole blanket together, then using needle B, pick up and k 20sts across each square along one side.
NEXT ROW: K1fb, k to end.

Rep last row until the border is the required length. The blanket shown on page 132 has 4 rows. Cast off. Rep for each side of the blanket. Whipstitch the mitered corners together.

Finishing

Weave in all yarn ends with a darning needle. If desired, block the blanket (see p.238) according to the ballband instructions and be careful not to flatten the stitches.

top tip

Use up any leftover aran or DK yarn to make this colorful blanket.

Snowflake pillow

Impress your friends and family with your knitting skills with this distinctive and supersoft pillow, with its repeating snowflake motif in several coordinated colors and its bobble edging. Unusually for a Fair Isle project, it's worked in a super-chunky yarn on big needles.

❋ you will need

DIFFICULTY Moderate

SIZE 14 x 20in (35 x 50cm)

YARN
Plymouth Yarn DeAire 100g

A x 3   **B** x 1   **C** x 1   **D** x 1

NEEDLES
1 pair of US15 (10mm/UK000) needles

1 x US15 (10mm/UK000) 40in (100cm) long circular needle

GAUGE
9sts and 12rows over 4in (10cm) in st st

NOTIONS
Darning needle
2 x 1in (23mm) cream buttons
14 x 20in (35 x 50cm) pillow cushion, pins

SPECIAL ABBREVIATIONS
MB (Make bobble): Work up to MB. (k1, p1, k1) into next st, turn, p3, turn, k2tog, k1, pass first st over 2nd st. Cont as instructed.

◄ This pillow is knitted in Plymouth Yarn DeAire in A: 0100 Aspen, B: 0404 New England Nights, C: 0638 Annapolis, and D: 1662 Blue Mountain.

How to make

Front
With yarn A, cast on 59sts.
Work rows 1–38 using the chart, repeating sts 3–20 three times across the row.
Work the design in st st (k all RS rows and p all WS rows), stranding the colors not in use on WS (see p.215).
Cast off.

Back
The pillow back is worked in two pieces.

With yarn A, cast on 31sts.
ROW 1: K to end.
ROW 2: P to last 5sts, k5.
Rep rows 1 and 2 until piece measures 14in (35cm) from cast-on edge.
Cast off.
With yarn A, cast on 31sts.
ROW 1: K to end.
ROW 2: K5, p to end.
Rep rows 1 and 2 until piece measures 14in (35cm) from cast-on edge.
Cast off.

Supersized snowflake
The use of a chunky-weight yarn with large needles gives this motif a more modern feel.

Bobble edging strip

Knit the bobble edging in one long strip to go around all four edges. With yarn A, cast on 168sts.

ROW 1: K1, *MB, k3, rep from * to 3sts from end, MB, k2.

ROW 2: P to end.

Cast off loosely.

Finishing

Block (see p.238) all of the pieces. Lay out the cover front, RS up. Pin the bobble strips, RS facing, to the edges of the front pieces, with the cast-off edge of the strip lined up with the outer edge of the front.

Lay the back pieces on top, RS down, with the cast-on edges over the cast-on edge of the front piece, overlapping the garter stitch edges in the middle.

Pin all the pieces together, then backstitch (see p.241) around all edges. Turn the cover right side out, then sew the buttons to the bottom layer of the overlapped section at center back, 5in (12cm) from the top and bottom edges. Insert a pillow cushion and ease the buttons through the knitted stitches in the layer above to secure.

Snowflake in detail Once you start knitting, you will find the rhythm of the repeating snowflake motifs (stitches 3 to 20).

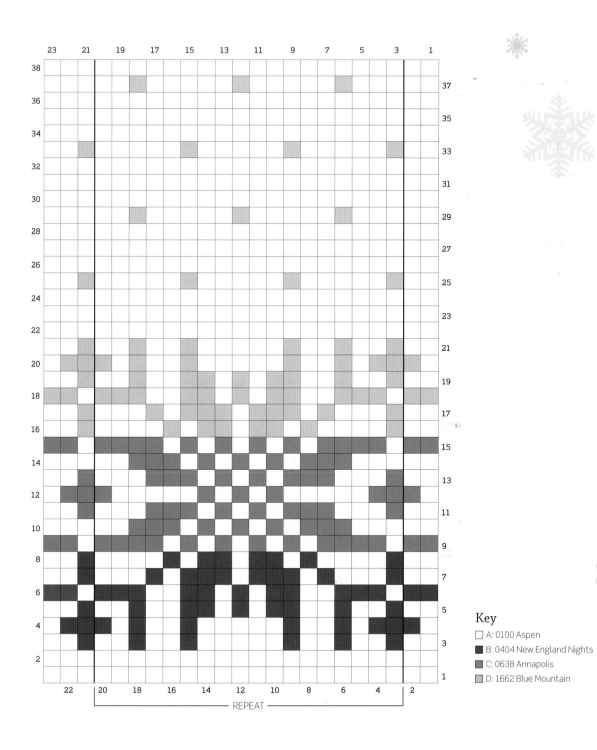

Key
☐ A: 0100 Aspen
■ B: 0404 New England Nights
■ C: 0638 Annapolis
☐ D: 1662 Blue Mountain

Fair Isle coasters

If you're itching to knit a Fair Isle piece but want to tackle charts and stranding of the colors first, then this is an ideal project to start with. The combination of colored yarns below will give you enough for two sets of four coordinated coasters.

How to make

Cast on 27sts.

The complete coaster can be worked from the chart alone, if preferred.

ROW 1 (RS): [K1, p1] to last st, k1.
Rep row 1 three times.

ROW 5: K1, [p1, k1] twice; k17, [k1, p1] twice, k1.

ROW 6: [K1, p1] twice; p19, [p1, k1] twice.
Rep rows 5 and 6.

ROW 9: K1, [p1, k1] twice; k17 joining in yarn B and working in Fair Isle as per chart row 9, [k1, p1] twice, k1. Take yarn B only to the extent of the Fair Isle pattern edge, leave it there, and collect it on the next row.

ROW 10: [K1, p1] twice; p19 as per next row of chart, [p1, k1] twice.

ROW 11: K1, [p1, k1] twice; k17 as per next row of chart, [k1, p1] twice, k1.
Rep rows 10–11 seven times.

ROW 26: Rep row 6.

ROW 27: Rep row 5.

ROW 28: Rep row 6.

ROW 29: Rep row 5.

ROW 30: [K1, p1] to last st, k1.
Rep row 30 three times.
Cast off.

◄ The coasters are made with Berroco Weekend in A: 5944 Starry Night, B: 5911 Tea Rose, and C: 5907 Mouse.

Finishing

Sew yarn ends of Fair Isle into the back of the coaster. Pin coaster square before blocking (see p.238) to the correct size.

Key

- ■ A: Starry Night
- ■ B: Tea Rose
- ▣ Purl on a RS row, knit on a WS row
- ▬ Knit on a RS row, purl on a WS row

Chart

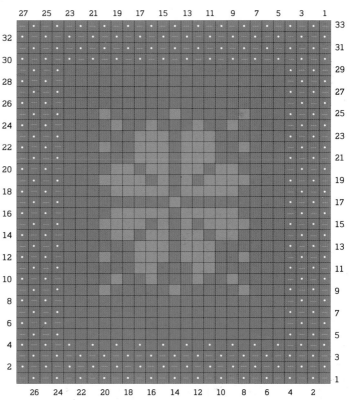

This beautifully textured pillow is perfectly accented on the back with wooden buttons.

Cabled pillow cover

This impressive pillow cover is knitted as one continuous piece—first the back, then the front, with the beautiful cable with the bobbles in the centers interspersed with strips of seed stitch. A textural masterpiece that is sure to be treasured.

How to make

Back
Cast on 73sts.
Work 9 rows in seed st.
Work in st st as follows, inc 1 st at center of first row. (74sts)
ROW 1: K.
ROW 2: K1, p to last st, k1.
Rep these 2 rows until work measures 13½in (34cm) from cast-on edge, ending with row 2.
NEXT ROW: K1, p to last st, k1. (This marks the bottom of the back.)
INC ROW (WS): K1 (p9, k4, p2, m1, p2, k4) 3 times, p9, k1. (77sts)

Front
ROW 1: K1, [(p1, k1) four times, p1, work 13sts row 1 cable with bobbles patt] 3 times, (p1, k1) 5 times.
These 2 rows set the patt for the seed st and cable panels.
Cont as set until front measures 16in (40cm), ending with a WS row.
DEC ROW: K1 [(p1, k1) 4 times, p1, p4, k1, k2tog, k2, p4] 3 times, (p1, k1) 5 times. (74sts)
NEXT ROW (WS): K 1 row. This marks the top fold line. Work in st st for 2½in

◄ This pillow cover is knitted in Debbie Bliss Blue Faced Leicester Aran in 14 Duck Egg.

(6cm), ending with a WS row, dec 1 st at center of last row. (73sts)
Work 4 rows seed st.
BUTTONHOLE ROW: Seed 5 (work 2tog, yo, seed 13) x 4, work 2tog, yo, seed to end.
Work 4 rows seed st.
Cast off.

Cable with bobbles
ROW 1: P4, T5L, p4.
ROW 2: K4, p2, k1, p2, k4.
ROW 3: P3, T3B, p1, T3F, p3.
ROW 4: K3, p2, k3, p2, k3.
ROW 5: P2, T3B, p3, T3F, p2.
ROW 6: K2, p2, k5, p2, k2.
ROW 7: P2, k2, p2, MB, p2, k2, p2.
ROW 8: As row 6.
ROW 9: P2, T3F, p3, T3B, p2.
ROW 10: As row 4.
ROW 11: P3, T3F, p1, T3B, p3.
ROW 12: As row 2.

Finishing
Block according to ballband instructions (see Blocking, p.238). With RS facing, sew side seams using mattress stitch (see p.239). Sew on buttons to correspond with the buttonholes.

This basket is knitted in a recycled fabric yarn—Hoooked Zpagetti — in Petrol.

Toy basket

Fabric yarns offer another world of knitting possibilities, especially for home accessories and bags. This recycled, jersey yarn knits up nicely into a softly shaped basket—use it for sorting toys, holding toiletries, or even serving bread at the dinner table.

you will need

DIFFICULTY Moderate

SIZE 12in (30cm) diameter x 11in (28cm) high

YARN
Hoooked Zpagetti 131yd (120m)

A x 1

NEEDLES
24in (60cm) long US17 (12mm) circular needle

GAUGE
11sts and 19 rows over 4in (10cm) in garter stitch

NOTIONS
Approx 60in (1.5m) of silky aran-weight yarn for provisional cast-on
Darning needle

SPECIAL ABBREVIATIONS
w&t (wrap and turn): s1 (the next resting loop) to RH needle, bring yarn to front, s1 back to LH needle, turn. Pull yarn lightly to ensure there is no excess yarn in the wrap.
When working a wrapped stitch on a subsequent row, ignore the wrap and work stitch as usual; the wrap blends in well with garter stitch.

How to make

The basket is worked in a single piece using short rows.
Provisionally cast on 37sts.
Working with the short length of the silky aran weight yarn, "provisionally" cast on an edge that you will unpick later on. (We used long-tail cast-on (see p.182).)
ROW 1: Change to main yarn, k.
ROW 2: K23, p1, k9, w&t.
ROW 3: K. (33sts)
ROW 4: K23, p1, k5, w&t.
ROW 5: K. (29sts)
ROW 6: K23, p1, k1, w&t.
ROW 7: K. (25sts)
ROW 8: K23, p1, k13.
These 8 rows form the repeat.
Work 20 repeats finishing the last repeat on row 7.
Graft (see p.240) the last knitted row to the first row following the instructions for row 8 and remove provisional cast-on.

Finishing
Be careful when finishing off the yarn ends because both sides of the basket are visible.

A stiffer basket If you'd like a less floppy basket, then insert a strip of cardboard to help it keep its shape.

Fair Isle Christmas ornaments

Add a handmade touch to the usual festive decorations with these Fair Isle ornaments. Whether they adorn the Christmas tree or are used decoratively on their own, as here, there are myriad color possibilities. You should get about five ornaments of each color from this yarn.

How to make

Using yarn A, cast on 10sts.

ROW 1 (RS): K1, [k1fb] x 8, k1. (18sts)

ROW 2: P.

ROW 3: K1, [k2, M1] x 8, k1. (26sts)

ROW 4: P.

ROW 5: K1, [k3, M1] x 8, k1. (34sts)

ROW 6: P.

ROW 7: K1, [k4, M1] x 8, k1. (42sts)

◀ These ornaments are made with Rowan Cotton Glacé in A: 725 Ecru, B: 858 Aqua, C: 741 Poppy, D: 859 Dark Forest.

ROW 8: P.

ROW 9: K1, [k5, M1] x 8, k1. (50sts)

ROW 10: P.

ROWS 11–25: Cont to work in st st, foll the chart incorporating yarn B while working the 6 stitch repeat 8 times in all across the row.

ROW 26: P.

ROW 27: K1, [k4, k2tog] x 8, k1. (42sts)

ROW 28: P.

ROW 29: K1, [k3, k2tog] x 8, k1. (34sts)

ROW 30: P.

ROW 31: K1, [k2, k2tog] x 8, k1. (26sts)

ROW 32: P.

ROW 33: K1, [k1, k2tog] x 8, k1. (18sts)

ROW 34: P.

ROW 35: K1, [k2tog] x 8, k1. (10sts)

Finishing

Break the yarn leaving a long yarn tail and thread that back through the 10 stitches and pull to create the top of the ornament, then stitch to secure. Repeat for the cast-on stitches.

Sew halfway up the ornament, then fill with poly fill.

Sew the ornament closed.

Key
☐ A: Ecru
▩ B: Aqua

Chart

❄
top tip
Try different colors that
complement each other.
Yellow and a rich purple
also work well.

Tools & Equipment

Yarns

There are many types of yarns, allowing knitters to enjoy a variety of sensory experiences as they express themselves through the medium. Yarns can be made of many different fibers and have a range of textures, as shown here.

Fibers

Yarns, like fabrics, are made from fibers. A fiber may be the hair from an animal, man-made (synthetic), or derived from a plant. The fibers are processed and spun to make a yarn. A yarn may be made from a single type of fiber, such as wool, or mixed with other fibers to enhance its attributes (for example to affect its durability or softness). Different blends are also created for aesthetic reasons, such as mixing soft, luxurious cashmere with a rougher wool. As a result, all yarns have different properties, so it is important to choose an appropriate blend for the project at hand.

WOOL

The hair, or fleece, of a variety of breeds of sheep, such as the Shetland Moorit or Blue Faced Leicester, is made into pure wool yarns or blended with other fibers. It is very warm and durible, and great for winter wear such as jackets, cardigans, hats, and gloves. Some wool is rough, but softens with wear and washing. Wool sold as "organic" contains a high proportion of lanolin, making a strong, waterproof yarn.

MERINO WOOL

This is wool derived from the merino sheep, which is said to provide one of the softest wools of any sheep breed. The bouncy, smooth-surfaced fiber is just as warm as a more wiry, coarse wool. Merino is a fantastic choice for wearing against the skin, and it is often treated to make it suitable for machine-washing. Merino wool is good for soft scarves, arm warmers, and children's garments.

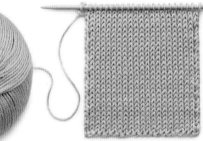

MERCERIZED COTTON

Cotton fiber can be mercerized, a treatment during which it undergoes mechanical and chemical processing to compress it and transform it into an ultra-strong yarn with a reflective sheen. It is a fine choice of fiber for a project that needs to be strong and hold its shape, such as a shiny evening bag, a long summer cardigan, or a throw.

SILK

The silkworm, a caterpillar that eats mulberry leaves, spins a cocoon to develop into a moth. It is from the fibers of the cocoon that silk is made. Silk is shiny and sleek, very delicate, and because of its extraordinary source, very expensive. The luxurious texture of silk yarn makes it ideal for wedding and christening gifts, and for indulgent, fitted knitwear.

ACRYLIC

Acrylic fibers are produced from ethylene, which is derived from oil, and they are inexpensive to manufacture. Acrylic yarns can feel slightly rougher than other synthetics, and they often come in bright and luminous shades, which are harder to create with natural fibers. Robust and resistant to moths, acrylic yarn is ideal for toys, novelty items, and budget projects. The yarn does tend to accumulate static electricity.

NATURAL AND SYNTHETIC MIXES

Man-made fibers are often blended with natural ones to provide structure, strength, and washability. These synthetics help to bind delicate fibers, such as mohair and cashmere. Some synthetic fibers provide "loft," and their inclusion can reduce cost while still offering a luxury fiber yarn. The strength of blends such as wool/nylon makes them perfect for socks and gloves.

Specialty yarns for textural effects

For knitters who love something a bit different, specialty yarns make life very exciting. From velvety chenille to yarns with different and irregular textures, there are lots of yarns to experiment with. Each yarn creates a different effect when knitted into a fabric, perhaps even looking like a fabric that has not been knitted at all! Read this section to bring out your inner textile artist, and let the yarns inspire you to create something that is fresh and edgy.

CHENILLE

This yarn is often composed of cotton and synthetics and is made up of short fibers emerging from a strong core. A fabric knitted in it will have a luxurious, velvety feel. Chenille is ideal for a plain stockinette stitch, but less so for intricate patterns and for work such as lace and cables, since it can hide the detail. It is a delicate yarn, which is likely to deteriorate with heavy wear and tear. It is therefore most suitable for plain-knitted garments for adults, and hats and scarves.

PLIED YARN

Most traditional yarn is made from more than one strand of spun fiber. "Ply" indicates the number of these strands twisted (plied) together in a yarn (i.e., 4-ply, 6-ply, or 8-ply). Plied yarns can contain several colors to give a mottled, tweedy effect. The yarn is widely available in a variety of fiber mixtures and is suitable for most knitting projects.

EYELASH YARN

When mixed in with other yarns, eyelash yarn is able to create a variety of effects, even resembling faux fur. This hairy yarn is an excellent choice for trims or edgings, looking like a machine-made fabric when knitted. It is a popular choice for scarves, and can be found in all sorts of forms, with combinations of metallic, ribbon, and silky "hairs" attached to a solid core.

SLUBBY YARN

This type of yarn is often spun by hand and is characterized by a varying thickness along its length. This mixture of thick and thin areas creates a unique, uneven, and what some would call "lumpy" fabric when knitted. The texture produced by slubby yarn makes unusual accessories and outerwear, such as jackets, and it can also be used to make sweaters

BRAIDED YARN

Two or more fibers are blended together to make a braided yarn. It often has a soft fiber, such as wool or cotton, for the core, which is then wrapped in a fiber such as nylon or a metallic blend. The mixture of fibers improves stitch definition: stitches are individually highlighted by the wrapping fiber around the core yarn.

RIBBON YARN

The shape of ribbon yarn is similar to that of tape yarn, but usually a bit wider. Both yarns often comprise synthetic or plant-fiber blends, to give them strength and sheen. Ribbon yarn lends itself especially well to making pretty accessories such as unique evening bags, scarves, and belts. It is also suitable for summer tops. Many ribbon and tape yarns are slippery, and special attention must be paid to gauge and handling.

TWEED YARN

The term "tweed" describes a classic fiber mixture in both yarns and woven cloth. Tweed is most often composed of natural wool fibers spun with intermingled flecks of contrasting colors. The first tweeds were made of undyed cream wool and undyed wool from another breed of sheep with darker hair to create a cream yarn with brown or black flecks, most recognizable in traditional aran or fisherman's sweaters. Now tweed yarns come in a variety of colors with an assortment of contrasting flecks, from bright to subtle, for a knit with layers of artistic interest.

TAPE YARN

The main characteristic of tape yarn is its flat shape. It may also be tubular and is flattened when wound into a ball. A fabric knitted in it varies, depending on whether you twist the yarn when knitting, or lay it flat over the needle when working each individual stitch. Twisting it will produce a nubbly fabric, while laying it flat will produce a smooth surface on the finished item.

BOUCLÉ YARN

The curly appearance of bouclé yarn results from whirls of fiber attached to a solid core yarn. When knitted, these loops of fiber stand out and create a carpetlike looped fabric. (Bouclé is also the name of a type of fabric manufactured using a similarly spun yarn.) Bouclé yarns are unique and often specify a deceptively larger gauge guideline as a result of their overall thickness. Bouclé is a lovely choice for very simply shaped garments, or for adding interest to plain stockinette stitch knits by inserting an area using this yarn for an alternative texture.

LOOSE-SPUN YARN

This type of yarn is usually more aerated and less dense than a regular yarn because it is more loosely spun. When knitted, it is light and bouncy and very soft. Very thick yarns are often spun in this way to prevent knitted garments from feeling too heavy, or subsequently losing their shape when worn. These thick yarns are good for chunky, quick-to-knit accessories such as snoods and leg warmers.

Unusual yarns

Subvert the traditional image of knitting with these radical departures from the historic heritage of wool and the convenience of modern synthetic yarns. Expand your horizons from everyday knitting and venture into the worlds of jewelry, sculpture, rug making, furnishings, and even home furnishings such as bowls and boxes. What's more, you'll make something truly unique. Many materials can be used as yarns: here are some ideas to experiment with.

PLASTIC BAGS

Recycle plastic bags by cutting them into strips and joining these together with tight knots to form yarn. Create interesting textures by mixing colored and clear bags; the knots will add further texture. Knit with a large needle, depending on the width of the strips you have cut— US15 (10mm/UK000) upward is recommended; also choose the size according to whether you want a very tight or a floppy plastic fabric. Use this technique to make bags, mats, and waterproof items such as toiletry bags or garden seat covers.

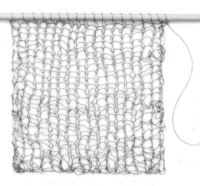

WIRE

This unusual medium is often used for knitting jewelry: buy beading wire, which is available in a range of colors, and knit it into chokers, necklaces, and bracelets. Try stranding beads on the wire before you work and place them in the knitting as you go along. For a really unusual project, strand the wire with another yarn to knit a malleable fabric that holds its shape and make three-dimensional sculptures.

STRING

Ideal for knitting practical household items, such as bowls and boxes, string is available in a range of colors and weights. Experiment with relatively small needles, such as US8 (5mm/UK6), to create a very stiff fabric capable of holding its shape. Coat finished household items with diluted craft glue to waterproof them and make future cleaning easy: just wipe with a damp cloth.

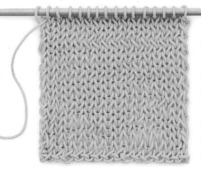

JELLY YARN

Also known as "rubber yarn," jelly yarn is used to make decorative accessories, such as belts, and three-dimensional sculptures. It is available in fluorescent, glittery, and glow-in-the-dark versions. The yarn may stick to knitting needles, so work with plastic or metal needles and use a lubricant such as baby oil. If the yarn has a hollow core, you can insert wire to make your work hold its shape.

FABRIC YARN

Traditionally, fabric from old clothes and other textiles was made into doormats and rugs by tying strips together; such recycled fabric yarn is also available to buy now, but you can make your own from knotting together fabric strips. The needle size will depend on how wide the strips are. Some knitters have even employed a pair of broom handles to knit very wide strips of raffia into hugely chunky and robust mats!

Buying yarn

Yarns are packaged for sale in different ways. It is most common for knitting yarn to be sold in balls, hanks, or skeins. Larger quantities of yarn come in cones, although these are most commonly sold for maching knitting and weaving. The amount of yarn you get per ball, hank, or skein varies, and is usually measured in yards or grams.

BALL

The stock in a yarn store will consist mostly of balls of yarn. These are ready to use: just pull the yarn from the center to start knitting.

SKEIN

Similar to balls but an oblong shape, skeins also need no special preparation. Pull the yarn from the center, as with a ball, and keep the label in place as you work to ensure that the skein doesn't unravel completely.

BOBBIN

Fabric yarn may come on a bobbin or a cone and is basically one long, narrow strip of fabric. The yarn winds off the outside, so just find the end of the yarn and start knitting.

CONE

A cone may be awkward to carry around in a knitting bag, in which case the yarn is best wound into balls before you start knitting.

HANK

This twisted ring of yarn, also sometimes called a skein, needs to be wound into a ball before it can be used. You can do this by hand or by using a ball-winder. This gives you the opportunity to check that there are no knots or faults in the yarn as you wind it. Some yarns available as hanks consist of soft, delicate fibers, and these are best wound by hand.

Yarn labels

Everything you need to know about a yarn is on its label, also known as a ballband. It will include symbols that tell you how to knit with the yarn and how to clean it. Below is just a selection of the most common symbols. Always keep the ballbands: they are vital for identifying the yarn if you need to buy more. When matching new yarn, always buy the same dye-lot number as the original to prevent a difference in color in the finished item.

BALLBAND
A yarn label or ballband features information on the yarn's weight and thickness, a general gauge swatch, and which needle size is recommended for its use as well as washing guidelines.

SYMBOLS
Yarn manufacturers may use a system of symbols to give details of a yarn. These include descriptions of suitable needles and the required gauge.

YARN WEIGHT AND THICKNESS

RECOMMENDED NEEDLE SIZE

GAUGE OVER A 4IN (10CM) TEST SQUARE

SHADE/COLOR 520

SHADE/COLOR NUMBER

DYE LOT NUMBER 313

DYE LOT NUMBER

50g IN ACCORDANCE WITH BS984 APPROX LENGTH 100YDS (90M)

WEIGHT AND LENGTH OF YARN IN BALL

100% WOOL

FIBER CONTENT

MACHINE-WASH COLD

MACHINE-WASH COLD, GENTLE CYCLE

HAND-WASH COLD

HAND-WASH WARM

DO NOT BLEACH

DRY-CLEANABLE IN ANY SOLVENT

DRY-CLEANABLE IN CERTAIN SOLVENTS

DO NOT DRY-CLEAN

DO NOT TUMBLE-DRY

DO NOT IRON

IRON ON LOW HEAT

IRON ON MEDIUM HEAT

Yarn weights

The yarn "weight" refers to its thickness. Some yarns are spun by manufacturers to fall into what are considered as "standard" yarn weights, such as US sport and worsted and UK double-knitting (DK) and aran. These standard weights have long histories and will probably be around for some time to come. Even within these "standard" weights, however, there is slight variation in thickness, and textured novelty yarns are not easy to categorize by thickness alone.

When defining yarn weight, visual yarn thickness is only one of the indicators of its category. A yarn can look thicker than another yarn purely because of its "loft"—the air between the fibers and the springiness of the strands.

By pulling a strand of yarn between your hands, you can see how much loft it has by how much the thickness diminishes when the yarn is stretched.

The ply of a yarn is also not a simple indication of its thickness. Plies are the number of strands twisted together around each other in the opposite direction from which they were spun to form a strong, balanced yarn. A yarn with four plies can be very thick or very thin, depending on the thickness of each individual ply. The samples on the following page show what the yarns look like when knitted in stockinette stitch. The yarn weight names give the common US term(s) first, followed by the UK term(s).

❄ Standard yarn-weight system

Yarn-weight symbol and category names	0 Fingering	1 Sock	2 Sport	3 DK	4 Worsted	5 Chunky	6 Bulky
Types of yarns* in category	Fingering, lace, 2-ply,	Sock fingering, superfine, baby, 3-ply	Sport, 4-ply, fine, baby	DK, Double- knit, light worsted, 5-6-ply	Worseted, Aran, Afghan, 12-ply	Chunky, bulky, craft, rug, 14-ply	Bulky, super bulky, roving, super chunky, 16-ply and up
Knit gauge ranges in st st over 4in (10cm)**	33–40*** sts	27–32 sts	23–26 sts	21–24 sts	16–20 sts	12–15 sts	6–11 sts
Recommended needle in metric size range (in mm)	1.5–2.25	2.25–3.25	3.25–3.75	3.75–4.5	4.5–5.5	5.5–8	8 and larger
Recommended needle in US size range	0 to 1	1 to 3	3 to 5	5 to 7	7 to 9	9 to 11	11 and larger

Guidelines only
* The generic yarn-weight names in the yarn categories include those commonly used in the US and the UK.
** The above reflect the most commonly used gauges for specific yarn categories. The categories of yarn and gauge ranges have been devised by the Craft Yarn Council of America (YarnStandards.com).
***Ultra-fine lace-weight yarns are difficult to put into gauge ranges; always follow the gauge in your pattern for these yarns.

Knitting with different weights of yarn

FINGERING/LACE/2-PLY

Extremely light and often sold in a plentiful quantity. If worked on needles of the recommended size, the yarn produces a very fine-knit, delicate result. It can be more pleasurable to use the yarn with slightly larger needles for a more open fabric and a slightly quicker knit.

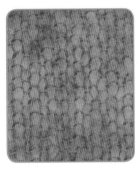

SOCK/BABY/3-PLY

An ideal choice for lightweight lace work. This yarn goes a long way per ball and requires very slim needles. A gossamer yarn such as this one highlights stitch definition and very fine detail, and intricate lace work looks stunning in it.

SPORT/4-PLY

Many knitters prefer fine to superfine, since it uses a more comfortable needle size yet still produces a very fine knit. This yarn is good for socks and baby clothes; the small stitches and neat appearance also suit items with designs that feature delicate texture or colorwork.

DK (DOUBLE-KNIT)/ LIGHT WORSTED/5–6 PLY

DK yarn is used for anything from blankets and toys to sweaters and cardigans. It is commonly associated with US6 (4mm/UK8) needles, and this slightly thicker alternative to 4-ply yarn knits up more quickly and may therefore be preferable to work with.

WORSTED/12-PLY

This thick and warm yarn commonly uses US8 (5mm/UK6) needles. It is good for men's garments with thick cabled detail, and the result is not too heavy. Ideal for functional items, many yarns in this thickness employ a large variety of fibers to make them machine-washable.

CHUNKY/14-PLY

Although bulky, the yarn mainly consists of lightweight fibers to prevent garments from drooping out of shape over time. Commonly worked on US10½ (7mm/UK2; see p.169) needles to create a chunky fabric for outerwear, hats, and leg warmers. Quick to knit; perfect for gifts.

BULKY/16 PLY+

The yarn thickness varies, but it is worked with large needles from US11 (8mm/UK0) upward, usually about US15 (10mm/UK000). A great choice for beginners, as stitches are so large that mistakes are easily visible. Knits up very quickly; good for rugged scarves.

Choosing yarn colors

When embarking on a new knitting project, the choice of color is a very important decision. Even a simple design gains impact from good color choices. The color wheel is a useful tool that will introduce you to color theory.

The color wheel: The three primary colors, red, yellow, and blue, form the basis of a color wheel. When two primary colors are combined, they create secondaries. Red and yellow make orange, yellow and blue make green, and blue and red make purple. Intermediate colors, called tertiaries, occur when a secondary is mixed with the nearest primary.

Complementary colors: Colors that lie opposite one another on the wheel, such as red and green, or yellow and violet, are called complementaries. They provide contrasts that accent design elements and make both colors stand out. Don't forget black and white—the ultimate opposites.

Hue, shade, tone, and tint: Each segment shows the hue, shade, tone, and tint of a color. A hue is the pure, bright color; a shade is the color mixed with black; a tone is the color mixed with gray; and a tint is the color mixed with white (pastels). The use of color can affect the appearance of a finished project dramatically.

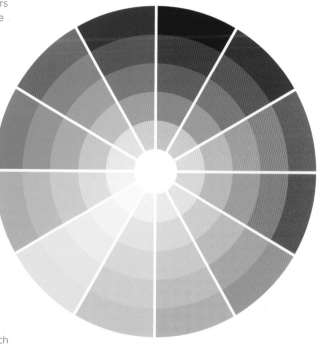

Monochromatic designs: These use different versions of the same color. So a project based on greens, for instance, will not stray into the red section of the color wheel, but might have shades and tints of yellow and blue mixed in, which can then become harmonious combinations of colors that are next to each other on the color wheel. These adjacent colors can also be combined to great effect, as long as there are visual differences between them.

Color temperature: Color has a visual temperature, with some colors being perceived as warm and others as cool. Many people tend to think of blue and its adjacent colors as being cool, while the reds and yellows are warm, but, in fact, there are warmer and cooler versions of all the primaries; think, for example, of a warm, azure blue and a cold, icy blue. Color temperature is an important element in whether a color recedes or advances—that is, in whether it blends in with or stands out from the background and any other surrounding colors.

Black and white

Black and white are not included on the color wheel because they are not classified as colors. Black is literally an absence of all color, and white is a combination of all colors in the spectrum. Bear in mind that when using black, not only is your work more difficult to see, but textural work will also not be seen to best effect in the final garment or work. White, however, guarantees that every stitch and detail will be clear; the drawback is that white shows smudges of dirt more quickly and therefore needs to be washed more frequently.

WARM SHADES

The warm end of the color spectrum consists mainly of red and yellow tones; browns, oranges, and purples are part of this group. Use these colors to bring richness and depth. A blend of warm shades can be a very flattering mixture to use, depending on your coloring: hold the yarn against your face to see what suits you.

COOL SHADES

Blue, green, and violet are at the cool end of the spectrum, and these can look very good used together. Cool colors are generally darker in tone than warm ones. If used with warm shades, their impact is lessened: if you need to balance a warm mixture in a project, you will need a higher proportion of cool colors than warm ones to do it.

PASTELS

These very pale, often cool variations of deeper, darker colors are very popular for babies' and small children's garments; consequently, a variety of suitable synthetic yarns and blends is available. Pastels also feature strongly in spring/summer knitting patterns for adults: look for ice-cream colors in lightweight yarns, and enjoy using a delicate color palette.

BRIGHTS

Vivid and fluorescent shades are fun to use in a project and often make particularly eye-catching accessories or color motifs. A great way to liven up a colorwork project that consists of muted shades is to add a bright edging or set of buttons. This burst of color can change the project's overall color impact completely.

SEASONAL MIXTURES

Nature can be a great source of inspiration. Think about sunsets, fall leaves, frosted winter berries, or vibrant spring flowers. Keep a record of these in a sketchbook or in photographs, and notice the proportion of each color in view. Most good yarn stores change their range of colors according to the season: in spring, for example, more pastels and brights will be available.

Knitting needles

Finding the right knitting needles is mostly down to personal preference. If you are a beginner, purchase a pair of quality US6 (4mm/UK8) needles and a ball of DK (double-knitting) wool yarn (see p.165) to learn and practice techniques with.

CABLE NEEDLE
A kinked or U-shaped cable needle is used when working cables; this shape prevents cable stitches from sliding away.

STRAIGHT KNITTING NEEDLES
Ordinary knitting needles with rigid shanks and a stopper at one end are called straight needles or pins. They come in a range of sizes (see the following page) and lengths. The most common material for straight needles is metal, like these. Metal needles have very good points and are extremely long-lasting.

BAMBOO KNITTING NEEDLES
Some knitters swear by bamboo needles and say that the loops of yarn slide beautifully along them. Wooden and bamboo needles have a natural flexibility and may help alleviate hand strain when knitting.

PLASTIC KNITTING NEEDLES
Plastic needles come in a range of attractive colors. Because they are inexpensive, special short ones are produced especially for children to learn to knit with.

JUMBO NEEDLES
Knitting needle sizes from US17 (12mm) upward are sometimes called jumbo needles. These needles are used for bulky yarns (see p.124) to make superfast sweaters or scarves as well as for knitting up fabric and plastic yarns (see p.146).

CIRCULAR NEEDLES

These have long or short plastic wire between the straight, stiff ends. Long circular needles are used for knitting very wide items (such as blankets or garments knitted in one piece) back and forth in rows, because very many stitches can be packed onto the wire. Knitting can also be worked around and around in a tube on circular needles, for example, sweaters are sometimes knitted in the round up to the armholes. Short circular needles are designed for tubular hats, neckbands, armhole bands, and sleeves, eliminating the need for seams. Interchangeable circular needles that work with a detachable cable are a popular alternative to buying each size separately.

☀ conversion chart

This chart gives the closest conversions between the various needle-size systems. The sizes don't match exactly in many cases but are the closest equivalents.

Metric	US	Old UK
1.5mm	000 00	N/A
2mm	0	14
2.25mm 2.5mm	1	13
2.75mm	2	12
3mm	NA	11
3.25mm	3	10
3.5mm	N/A	4
3.75mm	5	9
4mm	6	8
4.5mm	7	7
5mm	8	6
5.5mm	9	5
6mm	10	4
6.5mm	10½	3
7mm	N/A	2
7.5mm	N/A	1
8mm	11	0
9mm	13	00
10mm	15	000
12mm	17	N/A
15mm	19	N/A
20mm	35	N/A
25mm	50	N/A

DOUBLE-POINTED NEEDLES

Designed so that stitches can be slipped on and off both ends, double-pointed needles—or dpns, for short—are used for circular knitting (see pp.224-227), for certain fancy color stitch patterns, and for knitting cords.

Other equipment

Hundreds of different gadgets are available to knitters. Some are merely for convenience, whereas others are absolutely vital and perform specific tasks. Each knitter will favor certain types of gadget over others, but these basic items should always be on hand when you are working on a project. Most knitters store their equipment in a portable knitting bag or case so it is easy to take everything along wherever they want to sit and knit. The tools below are relatively inexpensive and can be purchased from craft stores and yarn shops.

KNITTING NEEDLE GAUGE

Many knitting needles, such as double-pointed needles, circular needles, interchangeable needles, and vintage needles are not marked with a size. It is vital to know what size a needle is, so poke it through the holes in the gauge to find out. Many also feature a ruler, which you can use to measure gauge swatches.

TAPESTRY OR DARNING NEEDLE

This is used for sewing in the ends of yarn, sewing up seams, and attaching buttons or trimmings.

SCISSORS

Keep a pair of good-quality scissors on hand for cutting yarn and trimming ends. Sharp, short-bladed scissors are perfect: they allow you to snip very close to the work and so trim darned-in ends neatly when finishing a seam.

PINS

The large heads on pins prevent them from getting lost. Use them to pin pieces of knitting together when finishing work, as well as to pin work out to the correct measurements when blocking.

STITCH HOLDERS

These are used to hold stitches that you will return to later. You can make your own stitch holder from a length of lightweight cotton yarn, a safety pin, or a paper clip.

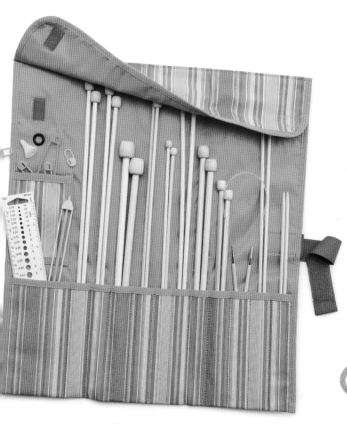

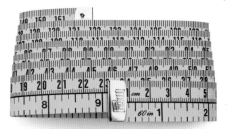

TAPE MEASURE

Use this to measure the person you are knitting for, and for gauging sizing accurately. Also use it to check gauge and measure knitting. Use either US or metric measures, never a mixture of both.

STITCH MARKERS

Use these to mark the beginning and end of a panel of stitches, and to identify the end of each row when working in the round. As you arrive at a marker, transfer it from the right-hand to the left-hand needle; continue working the row as normal.

NEEDLE ORGANIZER

Use this to keep your knitting needles organized and protected against damage. Needle rolls and bags are available in a range of shapes and sizes. Keep tapestry needles in a long pencil-caselike bag along with circular needle cables; double-pointed needles can be stored in a short needle roll.

KNITTING BAG

Bags for knitters often have many compartments, perfect for storing equipment and materials for your current project. To protect knitting from damp and moths, keep a cedar cube inside.

ROW COUNTER

Available as a tube that sits at the end of a knitting needle: change the counter when you complete a row; also available as a clicker that you "click" each time you finish a row.

POINT PROTECTORS

Place these over fragile needle tips to guard against damage; use them to protect your knitting bag from holes; and to stop stitches from sliding off needles and unraveling when not in use.

Techniques

Key techniques

Learning to knit is a very quick process. There are only a few key skills to master before you are ready to create simple shaped items, such as scarves, baby blankets, pillow covers, and throws. The knitting basics include casting stitches onto the needle, the knit and purl stitches, and casting (or binding) the stitches off the needles to finish the work.

Making a slipknot

Before you can start knitting, you must first learn how to place the first loop on the needle. This loop is called the slipknot and it is the first stitch formed when casting on stitches.

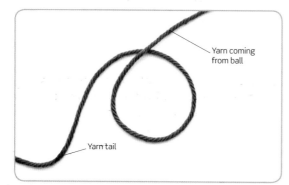

Yarn coming from ball

Yarn tail

1 Begin by crossing the yarn coming from the ball over the yarn end (called the yarn tail) to form a circle.

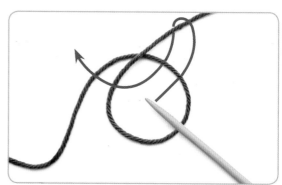

2 Insert the tip of a knitting needle through the circle of yarn, then wrap the needle tip around the ball end of the yarn and pull the yarn through the circle.

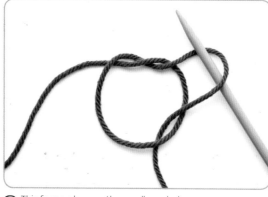

3 This forms a loop on the needle and a loose, open knot below the loop.

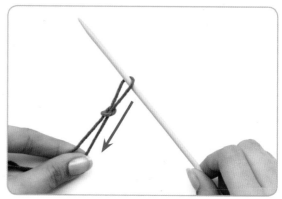

4 Pull both ends of the yarn firmly to tighten the knot and the loop on the needle.

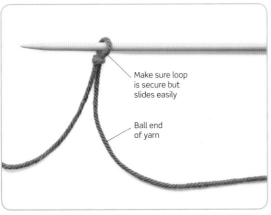

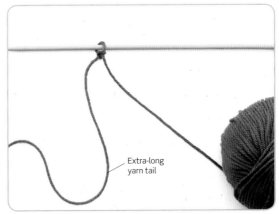

5 Make sure the completed slipknot is tight enough on the needle that it won't fall off but not so tight that you can't slide it along.

6 The yarn tail should be at least 4–6in (10–15cm) long so it can be darned in later. Your knitting pattern, however, may instruct you to leave an extra-long yarn tail (called a long loose end) to use for seams or other purposes.

Holding yarn and needles

Although all knitting is formed in exactly the same way, you can hold the yarn in either the right hand or the left hand. These two yarn-holding techniques are called the "English" and "Continental" methods. Knitting is ambidextrous, so right-handed and left-handed knitters should try both knitting styles to see which one they prefer.

Knitting "English" style

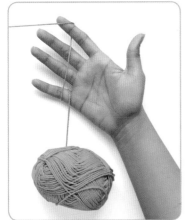

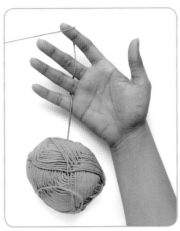

1 The yarn is laced around the fingers of the right hand. Aim to control the yarn firmly but with a relaxed hand, releasing it to flow through the fingers as the stitches are formed.

2 Try this alternative technique as well or make up your own. You need to hold the yarn just tautly enough with your fingers to create even loops that are neither too loose nor too tight.

3 Hold the needles with the stitches about to be worked in the left hand and the other needle in the right hand. Use the right forefinger to wrap the yarn around the needle.

Knitting "Continental" style

1 Lace the yarn through the fingers of the left hand in any way that feels comfortable. Try both to release and tension the yarn easily to create uniform loops.

2 In this alternative technique, the yarn is wrapped twice around the forefinger.

3 Hold the needle with the unworked stitches in the left hand and the other needle in the right hand. Position the yarn with the left forefinger and pull it through the loops with the tip of the right needle.

Alternative "Continental" style knitting

This alternative "Continental" method makes knit stitches very easy, and it is ideal for garter or circular stockinette stitch. As you work right near the tip, short tapered needles are best if you find that this method suits you. When knitting Continental style you may find your tension loosens, in which case step down a needle size or two, as necessary.

Alternative "Continental" knit Stitch

For both the knit and the purl stitches, wrap the yarn around your left little finger, but keep it over all your fingers. This makes purling easier.

1 Hold your index finger up with the yarn over it and use the pad of your middle finger to hold the yarn against the left needle, slightly forward of the stitch.

2 Insert the right tip into the stitch, pull and catch the yarn on your middle finger, draw it through the stitch on the left needle and off. At the end of the row, keep the yarn around your left fingers. Swap the needles to start the next row.

Alternative "Continental" purl stitch

1 Hold the yarn as for the knit stitch. Bring the yarn to the front. With your index finger raised and your middle finger touching the left needle near the tip, insert the needle as for a purl. Tilt the right tip toward you and then back in a small circular movement so that the yarn wraps over it.

2 At the same time, bring your left index finger with the yarn on it forward, wrapping the yarn around the needle. Keep your index finger in constant contact with the left needle.

3 Immediately dip the right needle tip slightly away from you to hook the yarn and pull the old stitch open. Take the needle backward through the old stitch and make a new purl loop. Slide the old stitch off the left needle.

Alternative "Continental" purl stitch—untwisting an incorrect stitch

1 If the front "leg" of the stitch is farther back along the needle than the back "leg" of the stitch, it is twisted.

2 To untwist the stitches on the following row, simply knit into the back of the stitch. If you find it difficult to master the correct wrap, but still wish to purl in the "Continental" style, then work every knit row following a purl row by working into the back of the stitch.

Winding up a long yarn tail

A long loose end on your slipknot can start to get tangled when it is packed away. To keep it neat, wind it into a yarn "butterfly" close to your knitting.

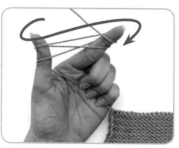

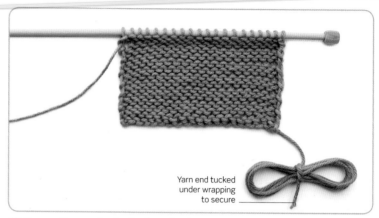

Yarn end tucked under wrapping to secure

1 Starting close to the knitting, wrap the yarn around your thumb and forefinger in a figure eight.

2 Remove the yarn "butterfly" from the thumb and forefinger, and wrap the yarn end a few times around its center. Tuck the end under the wrapping to secure it.

Single strand cast-ons

These cast-ons are all related to the backward loop cast-on and use one strand. They are soft, but can be firmed up by twisting. Alternating loop cast-on makes a decorative edge. Casting on knitwise and cable cast-on are useful for casting on in the middle of a piece, for example, if you need to add more than one stitch when increasing. When followed by stockinette stitch, casting on knitwise can curl toward the knit side. If this matters, choose a two-strand tubular cast-on (see p.185).

Backward loop cast-on (also called *thumb or single cast-on*)

Yarn tail

Yarn going to ball

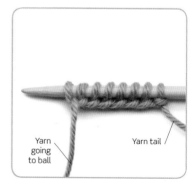

Yarn going to ball

Yarn tail

1 Hold the needle with the slipknot in the right hand. Then wrap the yarn around the left thumb and hold it in place in the palm of the left hand. Insert the needle tip under and up through the loop on the thumb, following the arrow.

2 Release the loop from the thumb and pull the yarn to tighten the new cast-on loop on the needle, sliding it up close to the slipknot.

3 Loop the yarn around the thumb again and continue making loops in the same way until the required number of stitches is on the needle.

Knit-on cast-on (also called *knit-stitch cast-on*)

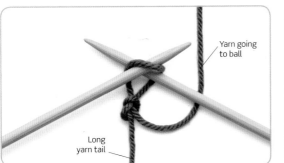

1 Holding the yarn in the left or right hand as explained on p.175, place the needle with the slipknot in the left hand. Then insert the tip of the right needle from left to right through the center of the loop on the left needle.

2 With the yarn behind the needles, wrap it under and around the tip of the right needle. (While casting on, use the left forefinger or middle finger to hold the loops on the left needle in position.)

3 With the tip of the right needle, carefully draw the yarn through the loop on the left needle. (This is the same way a knit stitch is formed, hence the name of the cast-on.)

4 Transfer the loop on the right needle to the left needle by inserting the tip of the left needle from right to left through the front of the loop.

5 Pull both yarn ends to tighten the new cast-on loop on the needle, sliding it up close to the slipknot.

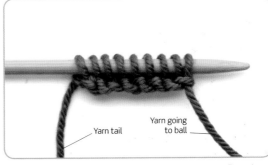

6 Continue casting on stitches in the same way until you have the required number of stitches. For a looser cast-on, hold two needles together in your left hand while casting on.

Cable cast-on

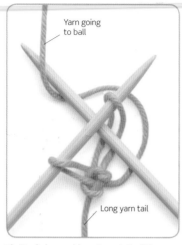  

Yarn going to ball

Long yarn tail

1 Begin by working steps 1–5 of the knit-on cast-on (see p.179). Then insert the tip of the right needle between the two loops on the left needle and wrap the yarn under and around the tip of the right needle.

2 With the tip of the right needle, draw the yarn through to form a loop on the right needle.

3 Transfer the loop on the right needle to the left needle (see step 4, p.179). Continue, inserting the needle between the first two loops on the left needle when beginning each new cast-on stitch.

Finger loop cast-on

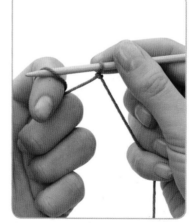 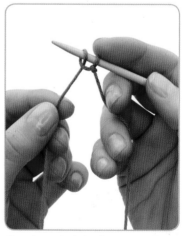

1 This technique gives a soft cast-on. Hold the needle with the skipknot in the right hand. Lift the yarn from underneath with your left index finger pointing away from you. Bend and turn your finger to point toward you.

2 Insert the needle into the loop that lies on top of the finger from behind.

3 Release the index finger and tighten the stitch on the needle.

Alternating loop cast-on

 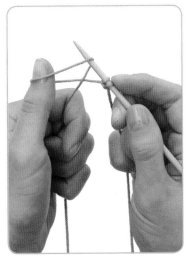 

1 Work the first stitch as for finger loop cast-on, as shown the previous page.

2 Work the second stitch as backward loop cast-on by lifting the yarn from behind with the left thumb, winding it around the thumb and inserting the needle into the front strand (see p.178).

3 Repeat steps 1 and 2 to cast on as many stitches as you need. On the first row, work into the front of the stitches, even if they look twisted.

Double twist loop cast-on

This is firmer than backward loop cast-on, and the first row is easier to knit.

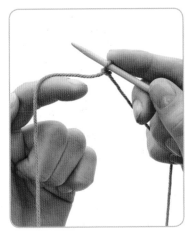  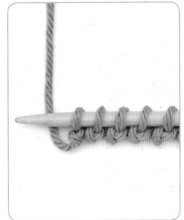

1 Hold the needle with the skipknot in your right hand. Lift the yarn from behind with your left index finger.

2 Twist the yarn by twirling your finger twice in an counterclockwise circle. Place the loop from your finger on the needle and pull to tighten.

3 Repeat steps 1-2 to cast on as many stitches as you need. The resulting decorative edge is open textured.

Long-tail cast-on (also called *double cast-on*)

1 Make a slipknot on the needle, leaving a very long yarn
tail—allow about 1⅜in (3.5cm) for each stitch being cast on.
Hold the needle in your right hand. Then loop the yarn tail over
the left thumb and the ball yarn end over the left forefinger as
shown. Hold both strands in the palm of the left hand.

Labels on image: Long yarn tail / Yarn going to ball

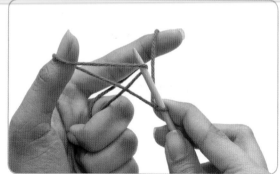

2 Insert the tip of the needle under and up through the
loop on the thumb.

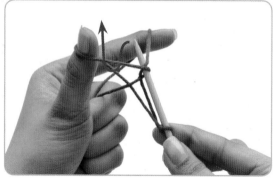

3 Wrap the tip of the needle around the loop on the forefinger
from right to left and use it to pull the yarn through the loop
on the thumb as shown by the large arrow.

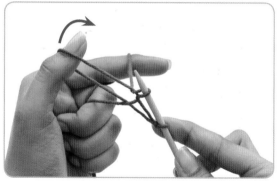

4 Release the loop from the thumb.

5 Pull both yarn ends to tighten the new cast-on loop on the
needle, sliding it up close to the slipknot.

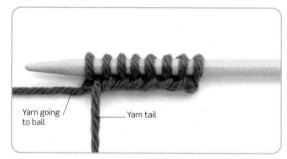

6 Loop the yarn around the thumb again and cast on
another stitch in the same way. Cast on as many stitches
as you need for your project.

Labels on image: Yarn going to ball / Yarn tail

Contrast-edge cast-on

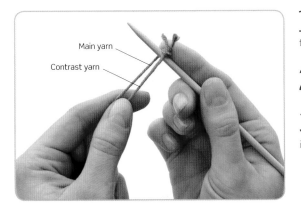

1 Cut a piece of contrast yarn three times the estimated length of the cast-on, and tie one end onto the end of the ball of the main colored yarn.

2 Hold both strands of yarn in your left hand, with the contrast yarn toward you and the knot at the end.

3 Slide the needle along between the yarns so that the knot sits snugly on the right side of the needle. Hold it in place with your right index finger.

4 Loop the contrast yarn over your thumb by moving it in a counterclockwise circle, and loop the main color over your index finger as shown. Insert the needle from below under the front strand of the contrast yarn on the thumb.

5 Move the needle toward your index finger and take the tip up and over the front index finger loop, pulling this back toward you, then pull this main color loop through the contrast-colored thumb loop.

6 Release the contrast yarn thumb loop. Pull both yarn ends to hold the needle snugly, and slide the cast-on stitch close to the slipknot.

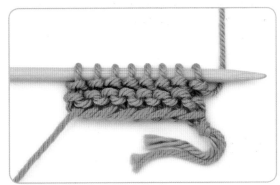

7 Repeat steps 4–6 to cast on the required stitches for your pattern. Knit the next row in the main yarn and continue working in garter stitch.

Twisted long-tail cast-on

This is stretchy, so it's useful before a rib. It can be made even stretchier by working it over two needles held together.

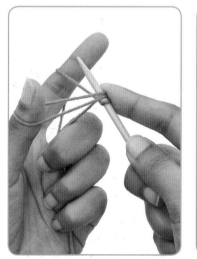

1 Hold the yarn and needle as for long-tail cast-on (see p.182). Bring the needle toward you and then back under both thumb loops.

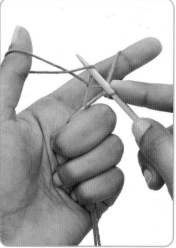

2 Bring the needle toward you over the top of the farthest thumb loop and down between both thumb strands. The thumb loop is now a figure eight.

3 Take the needle over the first loop on your index finger.

4 Bring the needle toward you. Drop the end of your thumb away from you and let the loop slide down toward the end to open the thumb loop. Bring the needle down through the open thumb loop.

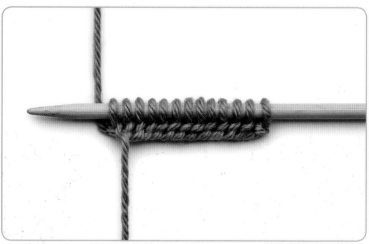

5 Release the thumb loop, keeping the yarn around your index finger ready to start the next cast-on loop. Pull the short strand to tighten the stitch.

6 Loop the yarn around the thumb again and repeat steps 1–4 to cast on another stitch in the same way. The stitches create a stretchy double-twist effect.

Tubular cast-on (also called *invisible cast-on*)

A good cast-on for single rib, but be wary of overstretching. Use needles at least two sizes smaller than for the main fabric.

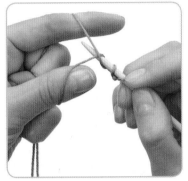

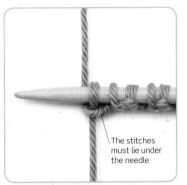

The stitches must lie under the needle

1 Hold yarn and needles as for long-tail cast-on (see p.182), but with the palm facing down, creating a "V" of yarn pointing to the right.

2 Bring the needle forward, passing over and back under the thumb strand. Catch the index-finger strand, going over and back toward you.

3 Turn your thumb away from you in a circular movement, flicking the thumb strand over the needle. Bring the left hand back to its original position, passing the yarn under the needle. Make sure that the stitch goes all the way around the needle and lies centrally under the needle.

4 Take the needle back over and under the index finger strand. With needle toward you, take it over and back under the thumb strand.

5 Move your index finger toward you in a circular movement, passing the yarn over the needle, and return your hand to its original position, making sure the stitch goes all the way around the needle. Repeat steps 2–5 to cast on an even number of stitches.

6 At the end, tie the strands together under the needle. Knit the first row by knitting into the back of the first stitch, bring the yarn to the front and slip the next stitch purlwise. Repeat along the row. For the second row, repeat but without knitting into the back of the stitch.

Joining on a new ball

End of old ball

New ball

Knot close to knitting

New ball joined on

1 Always join on a new ball at the beginning of a row. Knot the new end of yarn onto the old yarn.

2 Slide the knot up very close to the knitting. The knot can be hidden in the seam later. If you are knitting a scarf or blanket, tie the knot loosely so you can undo it later and weave in the ends.

Simple cast-offs

When your piece of knitted fabric is complete you need to close off the loops so that they can't unravel. This is called casting off (or binding off) the stitches. Although casting off is shown here worked across knit stitches, the principle is the same for purl stitches. If instructed to retain stitches for future use, slip them onto a spare needle or a stitch holder.

Casting off knitwise

1 Begin by knitting the first two stitches. Then insert the tip of the left needle from left to right through the first stitch and lift this stitch up and over the second stitch and off the right needle.

2 To cast off the next stitch, knit one more stitch and repeat step 1. Continue until only one stitch remains on the right needle. (If your pattern says "cast off in pattern," work the stitches in the specified pattern as you cast off.)

3 To stop the last stitch from unraveling, cut the yarn, leaving a yarn tail 8in (20cm) long, which is long enough to weave into the knitting later. (Alternatively, leave a much longer yarn end to use for sewing up a future seam.) Pass the yarn end through the remaining loop and pull tight to close the loop. This is called fastening off.

Slipping stitches off the needle

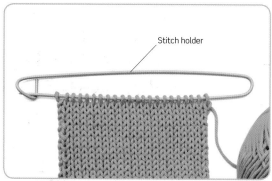

Stitch holder

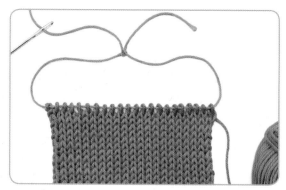

Using a stitch holder: If you are setting stitches aside to work on later, your instructions will tell you whether to cut the yarn or keep it attached to the ball. Carefully slip your stitches onto a stitch holder large enough to hold all the stitches. If you are only slipping a few stitches, use a safety pin.

Using a length of yarn: If you don't have a stitch holder or don't have one large enough, you can use a length of yarn instead. Using a blunt-ended darning needle, pass the yarn through the stitches as you slip them off the knitting needle. Knot the ends of the yarn together.

Alternative cast-offs

Try using one of these casting-off techniques to complement your project. Consider using a contrasting color, either in the basic cast-off or combined with a decorative style. Cast-offs are included here that give more stretch to ribs or loosen an edge, and an adaptation of the three-needle cast-off (see p.189) may even be used to join pockets and hems.

Purl cast-off

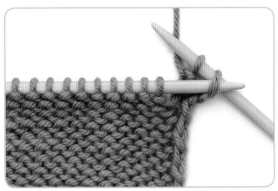 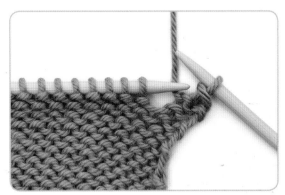

1 Purl two stitches, then take yarn to the back. Insert the tip of the left needle into the first stitch and pass it over the second stitch and off the right needle.

2 Bring the yarn to the front, repeat steps 1 and 2 across the row, but purl only one stitch in step 1. Pull the end stitch through itself as for casting off knitwise (see previous page).

Casting off in rib effect

Use after a single rib fabric to maintain the rib corrugations. This method adds a little more stretch than casting off in either all knit or all purl.

1 Work one knit and one purl. With the yarn at the back, insert the left needle into the first stitch. Pass over the second and off the right needle.

2 Knit the next stitch, then pass the first stitch over the second and off the right needle, as before.

3 With the yarn to the front, purl the next stitch. Repeat steps 2 and 3 across the row. Pull the final stitch through itself to fasten off.

Suspended cast-off (also called *delayed cast-off*)

This cast-off is ideal after lace knitting.

1 Knit the first two stitches (this starts the row and is not repeated). Insert the left needle tip into the first stitch and pass it over the second and off the right tip. Do not drop it from the left tip.

2 Bring the right needle across the front of the "suspended" stitch, and knit the first stitch on the left needle.

3 Slip both loops off together as you complete the knit stitch. Continue passing and knitting stitches as in steps 1 and 2 to the end of the cast-off.

Crochet cast-off

1 Hold the yarn in your left hand and keep it at the back. Slip the first stitch purlwise onto the crochet hook.

2 Insert the hook into the next stitch and drop it from the left needle. Catch the yarn with the hook and pull it through both of the stitches. Repeat across the row, pulling the end loop through itself to fasten off.

Three needle cast-off

This seam can be worked on the right side of the knitting (as here) to form a decorative seam, or on the wrong side.

1 Hold the needles with the stitches to be joined together with the wrong sides facing each other. Insert a third needle through the center of the first stitch on each needle and knit these two stitches together.

2 Continue to knit together one stitch from each needle as you cast off the stitches in the usual way. (A contrasting yarn is used here to show the seam clearly.)

3 When the pieces of knitting are opened out, you will see that this technique forms a raised chain along the seam.

Decrease cast-off

This decorative cast-off is better for single ribs than plain casting off knitwise.

1 Insert the tip of the right needle into the front of the first two stitches on the left needle and knit them together. Slip the new stitch on the right needle back onto the left without twisting it. Repeat across the row, pulling the thread through the last stitch to secure the end.

Knit stitch Abbreviation = k

All knitting is made up of two basic stitches—knit and purl. Choose backward loop, finger loop, or knit-on cast-on and start with garter stitch, where you knit every row (see p.192). Try fun stripes and experiment with different yarns before you learn the purl stitch (see following page). The odd dropped stitch doesn't matter; just put a safety pin through it so it does not drop farther and sew it in later. Knitting a row and then purling a row produces stockinette stitch, shown below (see also p.192). If you need to unpick a knit row or pick up a dropped stitch, see p.227.

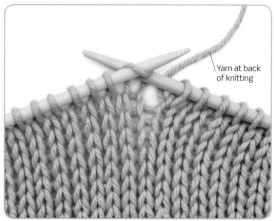

1 Hold the needle with the unworked stitches in your left hand and the other needle in your right hand, as explained on p.175. With the yarn at the back of the knitting, insert the tip of the right needle from left to right under the front loop and through the center of the next stitch on the left needle.

Yarn at back of knitting

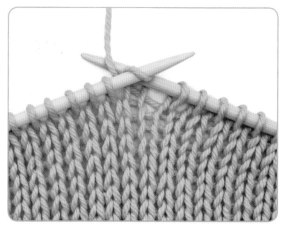

2 Wrap the yarn under and around the tip of the right needle, keeping an even tension as the yarn slips through your fingers.

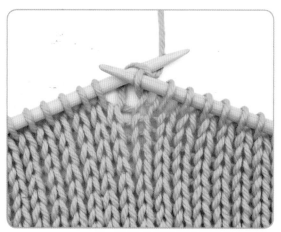

3 With the tip of the right needle, carefully draw the yarn through the stitch on the left needle. Hold the yarn firmly but not too tightly.

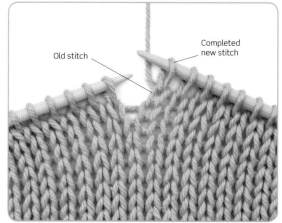

Old stitch

Completed new stitch

4 Let the old loop drop off the left needle to complete the knit stitch on the right needle. Work all the stitches on the left needle onto the right needle in the same way. To start a new row, turn the work around and transfer the right needle to the left hand.

Purl stitch Abbreviation = *p*

The purl stitch is a little more difficult than the knit stitch, but, like knit stitch, it becomes effortless after a little practice. Once you are a seasoned knitter, you will feel as if your hands would know how to work these basic stitches in your sleep. Work your first purl row after you have cast on and knitted a few rows of garter stitch. You may find that your tension alters on purl stitches, so try holding your yarn a little tighter or a bit looser to compensate. If you need to unpick a purl row or pick up a dropped stitch, see p.227.

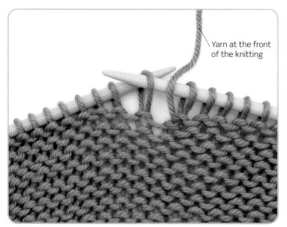

Yarn at the front of the knitting

1 Hold the needle with the unworked stitches in your left hand and the other needle in your right hand, as explained on p.175. With the yarn at the front of the knitting, insert the tip of the right needle from right to left through the center of the next stitch to be worked on the left needle.

2 As with the knit stitch, wrap the yarn over and around the tip of the right needle. Keep an even tension on the yarn as you release it through your fingers.

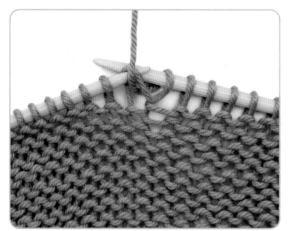

3 With the tip of the right needle, carefully draw the yarn through the stitch on the left needle. Keep your hands relaxed and allow the yarn to slip through your fingers in a gently controlled manner.

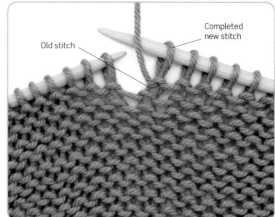

Old stitch

Completed new stitch

4 Let the old loop drop off the left needle to complete the purl stitch. Work all the stitches on the left needle onto the right needle in the same way. To start the next row, turn the work around and transfer the right needle to the left hand.

Basic knit and purl stitches

Once you know how to work knit and purl stitch with ease, you will be able to work the most frequently used stitch patterns—garter stitch, stockinette stitch, reverse stockinette stitch, and single ribbing. Stockinette stitch and reverse stockinette stitch are commonly used for plain knitted garments, and garter stitch and single ribbing for garment edgings. There is a world of textural patterns awaiting you that combine knit and purl stitches to great effect.

Garter stitch (Abbreviation = *g st*)

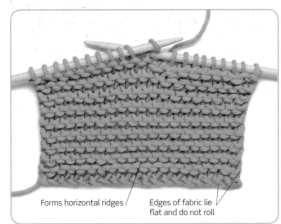

Forms horizontal ridges · Edges of fabric lie flat and do not roll

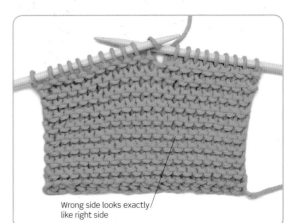

Wrong side looks exactly like right side

Knit right-side (RS) rows: Garter stitch is the easiest of all knitted fabrics because all rows are worked in knit stitches. When the right side of the fabric is facing you, simply knit all the stitches in the row.

Knit wrong-side (WS) rows: Again, knit all the stitches in the row. The resulting fabric is soft, textured, and slightly stretchy. Garter stitch works up slightly shorter than stockinette stitch, needing more rows than stockinette stitch to reach a given length.

Stockinette stitch (Abbreviation = *st st*)

Side edges roll slightly to back

Right side is smooth

Bottom edge naturally rolls up at front

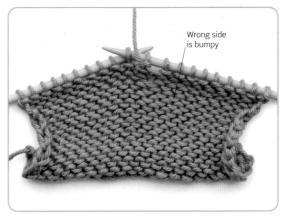

Wrong side is bumpy

Knit right-side (RS) rows: Stockinette stitch is formed by working alternate rows of knit and purl stitches. When the right side is facing you, knit all the stitches in the row.

Purl wrong-side (WS) rows: When the wrong side is facing you, purl all the stitches in the row. The wrong side is often referred to as the "purl side" of the knitting.

Reverse stockinette stitch (Abbreviation = *rev st st*)

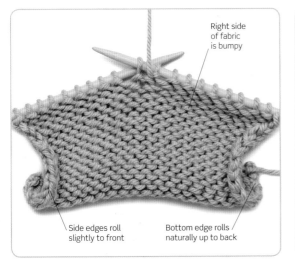

Right side of fabric is bumpy

Side edges roll slightly to front

Bottom edge rolls naturally up to back

Wrong side of fabric is smooth

Purl right-side (RS) rows: Reverse stockinette stitch is formed exactly like stockinette stitch but the sides are reversed. So, when the right side is facing you, purl all the stitches in the row.

Knit wrong-side (WS) rows: When the wrong side of the work is facing you, knit all the stitches in the row. Stockinette stitch and reverse stockinette stitch both roll at the ends and sides, whereas garter stitch and ribbing lie flat.

Single ribbing (Abbreviation = *k1, p1 rib*)

Ribbing has vertical ridges and is stretchy

Edges lie flat and do not roll

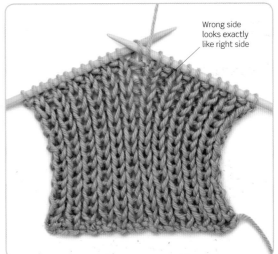

Wrong side looks exactly like right side

Right-side (RS) rows: Single ribbing is formed by working alternate knit and purl stitches. After a knit stitch, take the yarn to the front of the knitting between the two needles to purl the next stitch. After a purl stitch, take the yarn to the back between the two needles to knit the next stitch.

Wrong-side (WS) rows: On the wrong-side rows, knit all the knit stitches that are facing you and purl all the purl stitches. Over an even number of stitches, work the following rows in the same way to form thin columns of alternating single knit and single purl stitches.

Following stitch patterns

Stitch pattern instructions are written or charted directions for making all kinds of textures—knit and purl combinations, lace, and cables. Knitting stitch pattern swatches is the best possible introduction to row instructions. Beginners should try some before attempting to follow a complete knitting pattern (see p.196).

Understanding written instructions

Anyone who can cast on, knit and purl, and cast off can work from simple knit-and-purl-combination stitch pattern instructions with little difficulty. It is just a question of following the instructions one step at a time and getting used to the abbreviations. A list of common knitting abbreviations is given on the following page, but for simple knit and purl textures all you need to grasp is that "k1" means "knit one stitch," "k2" means "knit two stitches," and so on. And the same applies for the purl stitches—"p1" means "purl 1 stitch," "p2" means "purl 2 stitches," and so on.

To begin a stitch pattern, cast on the number of stitches that it tells you to, using your chosen yarn and the yarn manufacturer's recommended needle size. Work the row stitch by stitch, then repeat the rows as instructed and watch as the stitch pattern grows beneath the needles. When your knitting is the desired size, cast off in pattern (see pp.186–187).

The best tips for first-timers are to follow the rows slowly; mark the right side of the fabric by knotting a colored thread onto it; use a row counter to keep track of where you are (see p.171); and pull out your stitches and start again if you get confused. If you love the stitch pattern you are trying, you can make a scarf, blanket, or pillow cover with it—there is no need to buy a knitting pattern.

The principles for following stitch patterns are the same for cables (see p.213), which you will be able to work once you learn cable techniques and how to increase and decrease.

Some stitch patterns will call for "slipping" stitches and knitting "through the back of the loop." These useful techniques are given next as a handy reference when you are consulting the abbreviations and terminology list (see the following page).

Understanding stitch symbol charts

Knitting instructions for stitch patterns can also be given in chart form. Some knitters prefer working stitch symbol charts because they are easy to read, and they build up a visual image of the stitch repeat that is quick to memorize.

Even with charted instructions, there are usually written directions for how many stitches to cast on. If not, you can calculate the cast-on from the chart, where the number of stitches in the pattern "repeat" are clearly marked. Cast on a multiple of this number, plus any edge stitches outside the repeat.

Each square represents a stitch and each horizontal line of squares represents a row. After casting on, work from the bottom of the chart upward. Read odd-numbered rows (usually RS rows) from right to left and even-numbered rows (usually WS rows) from left to right. Work the edge stitches, then work the stitches inside the repeat as many times as required. Some symbols may mean one thing on a RS row and another on a WS row (see right).

Once you have worked all the charted rows, start again at the bottom of the chart to begin the "row repeat" once more.

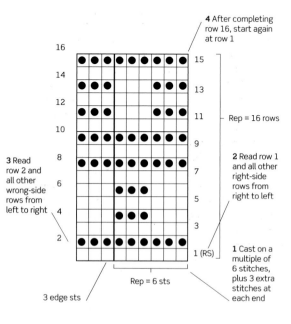

Knitting abbreviations

These are the most frequently used knitting abbreviations. Any special abbreviations in knitting instructions are always explained within the pattern.

alt	alternate
beg	begin(ning)
cm	centimeter(s)
cont	continu(e)(ing)
dec	decreas(e)(ing)
foll	follow(s)(ing)
g	gram(s)
g st	garter stitch
in	inch(es)
inc	increas(e)(ing)
k	knit
k1 tbl	knit st through back of loop
k2tog (or dec 1)	knit next 2 sts together (see p.204)
kfb (or inc 1)	knit into front and back of next st
LH	left hand
m	meter(s)
M1 (or M1k)	make one stitch (see pp.199-201)
mm	millimeter(s)
oz	ounce(s)
p	purl
p2tog (or dec 1)	purl next 2 sts together (see p.204)
patt	pattern, or work in pattern
pfb (or inc 1)	purl into front and back of next st (see p.199)
psso	pass slipped stitch over
rem	remain(s)(ing)
rep	repeat(ing)
rev st st	reverse stockinette stitch
RH	right hand
RS	right side (of work)
s	slip stitch(es)
s1 k1 psso (skp)	slip 1, knit 1, pass slipped st over (see p.205)
s1 k2tog psso (or sk2p)	slip 1 st, knit 2 sts together, pass slipped sts over (see p.205)
ssk	slip, slip, knit (see p.205)
s2 k1 p2sso	slip 2, knit 1, pass slipped stitches over (see p.206-207)
st(s)	stitch(es)
st st	stockinette stitch
tbl	through back of loop(s)
tog	together
WS	wrong side (of work)
yd	yard(s)
yo	yarn forward (UK yfwd; see p.203)
yo	yarn forward round needle (UK yfrn; see p.203)
yo	yarn over needle (UK yon; see p.203)
yo	yarn round needle (UK yrn; see p.202)
[ ] *	Repeat instructions between brackets, or after or between asterisks, as many times as instructed

Knitting terminology and symbols

The following terms are commonly used in knitting patterns. Where terminology differs between the US and UK, the UK equivalent is given in parentheses.

cast on Create a series of loops on a knitting needle to form the foundation for the piece of knitting.

cast off (bind off) Close off stitches and drop from knitting needle

cast off knitwise/purlwise Cast off while working stitches in knit/purl.

cast off in pattern Cast off while working stitches in the pattern used in the previous row.

cast off in ribbing Cast off while working stitches in the ribbing used in the previous row.

decrease Decrease the number of stitches in a row (see pp.204-207).

garter stitch Knit every row. In circular knitting (see p.224), knit one round and purl one round alternately.

gauge The size of the stitches in a piece of knitting (UK: tension), measured by the number of stitches and rows to 4in (10cm), or to 1in (2.5cm) on fine knitting.

increase Increase the number of stitches in a row (see pp.198-203).

knitwise Insert the right needle into the stitch on the left needle as if starting a knit stitch.

pick up and knit Draw loops through the edge of the knitting and place them on the needle (see p.228).

purlwise Insert the right needle into the stitch on the left needle as if starting a purl stitch.

stockinette stitch Knit all RS rows and purl all WS rows (UK: stocking stitch). In circular knitting (see p.224), knit every round.

reverse stockinette stitch Purl all RS rows and knit all WS rows (UK: reverse stocking stitch).

work even Work in specified pattern without increasing or decreasing (UK: work straight).

yarn-over increase Wrap yarn around right needle to make a new stitch; abbreviated yo (UK yfwd, yfrn, yon, or yrn; see pp.202-204).

STITCH SYMBOLS

These are some of the commonly used knitting symbols in this book. Any unusual symbols will be explained in the pattern. Symbols can vary, so follow the explanations in your pattern.

- □ k on RS rows, p on WS rows
- ● p on RS rows, k on WS rows
- ⊙ yarn-over (see p.202)
- ╱ k2tog (see p.204)
- ╲ ssk (see p.205)
- ⋀ sk2p (see p.205)
- ⋀ sk2 k1 p2sso (see p.206-207)

Following a pattern

The best advice for a beginner wanting to knit a first project from a knitting pattern is to start with a simple accessory. Pillow covers and scarves are the simplest because the instructions are straightforward and usually the only finishing details are seams. Below we look at an example of a pattern for a child's striped scarf (see pp.56–57).

At the beginning of most patterns you will find the skill level required for the knitting. Make sure you are confident that the skill level is right for you.

Check the size of the finished item. In some patterns, other sizes will be given in parentheses.

Try to use the yarn specified. But if you are unable to obtain this yarn, choose a substitute yarn as explained on p.164.

Instructions for working a piece of knitted fabric always start with how many stitches to cast on and what yarn or needle size to use. If there is only one needle size and one yarn, these may be absent here.

Familiarize yourself with any special abbreviations used in the pattern, such as for cabling. The more you knit the more abbreviations you'll become familar with—knitting books usually have a list of common ones (see p.195).

If no stitch is specified for the cast-off, always cast off knitwise.

CHILD'S STRIPED SCARF

Skill level
Easy

Size of finished scarf
To fit a child age 3–4 years, 5 x 37in (12 x 96cm)

Materials
4 x 50g balls of Debbie Bliss Rialto Aran in
A: 042 Sienna, B: 016 Ecru,
C: 043 Sunshine, and D: 010 Lime.
1 pair of US8 (5mm/UK6) needles
Darning needle

Gauge
19sts and 36 rows over 4in (10cm) in garter stitch US8 (5mm/UK6) needles or size necessary to achieve correct gauge.
With yarn A, cast on 22sts.
ROWS 1–10: Work in g st (k every st on every row).
ROWS 11–12: K in yarn B.
ROWS 13–14: K in yarn A.
ROWS 15–24: K in yarn B.
ROWS 25–26: K in yarn C.
ROWS 27–28: K in yarn B.
ROWS 29–38: K in yarn C.
ROWS 39–40: K in yarn D.
ROWS 41–42: K in yarn C.
ROWS 43–52: K in yarn D.
ROWS 53–54: K in yarn A.
ROWS 55–56: K in yarn D.
These 56 rows form the stripe rep.
Rep the stripe rep 6 times.
K 10 rows in yarn A.
Cast off. Then weave yarn ends.

Always purchase the same total amount in yards/meters of a substitute yarn; NOT the same amount in weight. Length information is on the ballband.

If desired, select different colors to suit the recipient; the colors specified are just suggestions.

Alter the needle size if you cannot achieve the correct gauge with the specified size (see below).

Making a gauge swatch before starting to knit the project is really important. Doing this ensures that the item will work up to the correct size. Change the needle size up or down, as necessary, to achieve the correct gauge.

Colors are usually changed on a right-side row, so end with the right side facing for the changeover row.

After all the knitted pieces are complete, follow the Finishing (or Making up) section of the pattern, if necessary.

See pp.239–241 for seaming options. Take time with seams on knitting. Practice on odd pieces of knitting before starting the main project.

Slipping stitches purlwise

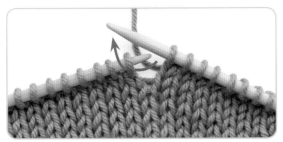

1 Always slip stitches purlwise, for example, when slipping stitches onto a stitch holder, unless instructed otherwise. Insert the tip of the right needle from right to left through the front of the loop on the left needle.

2 Slide the stitch onto the right needle and off the left needle without working it. The slipped stitch now sits on the right needle with the right side of the loop at the front just like the worked stitches next to it.

Slipping stitches knitwise

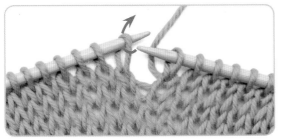

1 Slip stitches knitwise only if instructed to do so or if working decreases, as it twists the stitch. First, insert the tip of the right needle from left to right through the front of the loop on the left needle.

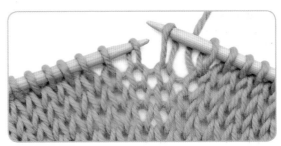

2 Slide the stitch onto the right needle and off the left needle without working it. The slipped stitch now sits on the right needle with the left side of the loop at the front of the needle unlike the worked stitches next to it.

Knitting through the back of the loop (Abbreviation = *k1 tbl*)

1 When row instructions say "k1 tbl" (knit one through the back of the loop), insert the right needle from right to left through the side of the stitch behind the left needle (called the back of the loop).

Crossed stitch

2 Wrap the yarn around the tip of the right needle and complete the knit stitch in the usual way. This twists the stitch in the row below so that the legs of the stitch cross at the base. (The same principle applies for working p1 tbl, k2tog tbl, and p2tog tbl.)

Increases and decreases

Increasing and decreasing the number of stitches on the needle is the way knitting is shaped, changing the edges from straight vertical sides to curves and slants. But increases and decreases are also used in combination with plain knit and purl stitches to form interesting textures in the knitted fabric, from lace to sculptured relief.

Simple increases

The following techniques are simple increases used for shaping knitting. They create one extra stitch without creating a visible hole and are called invisible increases.

Multiple increases, which add more than one extra stitch, are used less frequently and are always explained fully in the knitting pattern—one is given here as an example.

Knit into front and back of stitch (Abbreviation = *kfb* or *inc 1*)

This popular invisible increase for a knit row is also called a bar increase because it creates a little bar between the stitches.

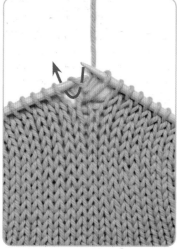

1 Knit the next stitch, leaving the stitch being worked on the left needle. Insert the right needle through the back of the loop from right to left.

2 Wrap the yarn around the tip of the right needle, draw the yarn through the loop to form the second stitch, and drop the old stitch off the left needle.

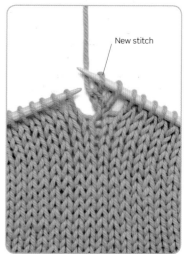

New stitch

3 Knitting into the front and back of the stitch creates two stitches from one and increases one stitch in the row.

Purl into front and back of stitch (Abbreviation = *pfb* or *inc 1*)

  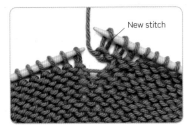

1 Purl the next stitch, leaving the stitch being worked on the left needle. Insert the right needle through the back of the loop from left to right.

2 Wrap the yarn around the tip of the right needle, draw the yarn through the loop to form the second stitch, and drop the old stitch off the left needle.

3 Purling into the front and the back of the stitch like this creates two stitches from one and increases one stitch in the row.

Lifted increase on knit row (Abbreviation = *inc 1*)

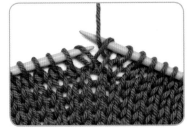  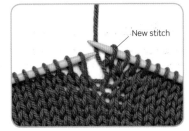

1 Insert the tip of the right needle from front to back through the stitch below the next stitch on the left needle. Knit this lifted loop.

2 Knit the next stitch (the stitch above the lifted stitch on the left needle) in the usual way.

3 This creates two stitches from one and increases one stitch in the row. (The purl version of this stitch is worked using the same principle.)

"Make-one" left cross increase on a knit row (Abbreviation = *M1 or M1k*)

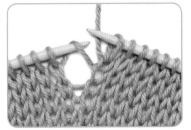  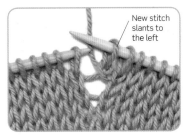

1 Insert the tip of the left needle from front to back under the horizontal strand between the stitch that has just been knitted and the next stitch. Then insert the right needle through the strand on the left needle from right to left behind the left needle.

2 Wrap the yarn around the tip of the right needle and draw the yarn through the lifted loop. (This is called knitting through the back of the loop.)

3 This creates an extra stitch in the row. (Knitting through the back of the loop twists the base of the new stitch to produce a crossed stitch that closes up the hole it would have created.)

"Make-one" right cross increase on a knit row (Abbreviation = *M1* or *M1k*)

Patterns do not always differentiate between left and right "make-one" increases.
Choose the most suitable for your project.

1 Insert the tip of the left needle from back to front under the
horizontal strand between the stitch just knit and the next
stitch. Insert the right needle from left to right into the front of
this new loop, twisting the stitch.

2 Wrap the yarn around the tip of the needle (in the usual
way) and draw the yarn through the lifted loop, knitting
into the front of the stitch.

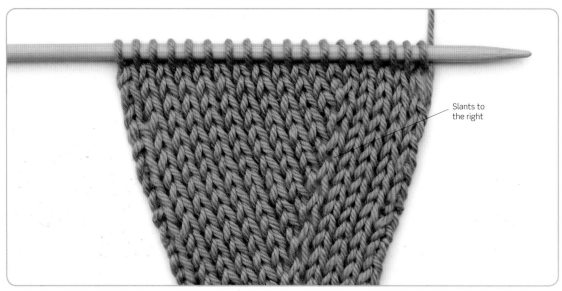

Slants to
the right

3 This action crosses the lifted stitch and closes the hole made by
picking up the loop. The resulting increase slants to the right and
is normally worked at the end of a knit row.

"Make-one" increase on a purl row (Abbreviation = *M1* or *M1p*)

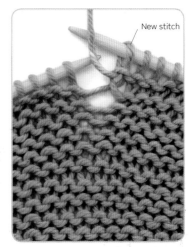

New stitch

1 Insert the tip of the left needle from front to back under the horizontal strand between the stitch that has just been knitted and the next stitch. Then insert the right needle through the strand on the left needle from left to right behind the left needle.

2 Wrap the yarn around the tip of the right needle and draw the yarn through the lifted loop (known as purling through the back of the loop.)

3 This creates an extra stitch in the row. (Purling through the back of the loop twists the base of the new stitch to produce a crossed stitch that closes up the hole it would have created.)

Multiple increases (Abbreviation = *[k1, p1, k1] into next st*)

Use this very easy increase if you need to add more than one stitch to an existing stitch, but be warned—it does create a small hole under the new stitches.

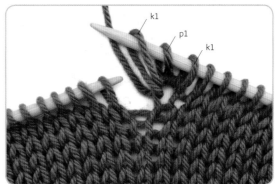

k1
p1
k1

1 To begin the increase, knit the next stitch but leave the old stitch on the left needle.

2 Then purl and knit into the same loop on the left needle (being sure to move the yarn to the front and then the back). This action is called knit one, purl one, knit one all into the next stitch. It creates two extra stitches in the row. You can keep alternating k and p stitches to create more stitches.

Yarn-over increases

Yarn-over increases add stitches to a row and create holes at the same time, so can be referred to as visible increases. They are used to produce decorative laces and openwork patterns in otherwise plain knitting. A yarn-over is made by looping the yarn around the right needle to form an extra stitch. It is important to wrap the loop around the needle in the correct way or it will become crossed when it is worked in the next row, which closes the hole.

Yarn-over between knit stitches (Abbreviation = *yo*)

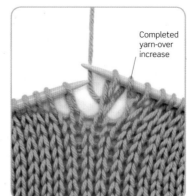
Completed yarn-over increase

Purl yarn-over on next row

1 Bring the yarn forward to the front of the knitting between the needles. Take the yarn over the top of the right needle to the back and work the next knit stitch in the usual way.

2 When the knit stitch is complete, the yarn-over is correctly formed on the right needle with the right leg of the loop at the front.

3 On the following row, when you reach the yarn-over, purl it through the front of the loop in the usual way. This creates an open hole under the purl stitch.

Yarn-over between purl stitches (Abbreviation = *yo*)

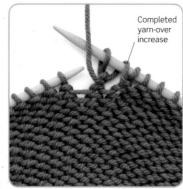
Completed yarn-over increase

Knit yarn-over on next row

1 Bring the yarn to the back of the work over the top of the right needle, then to the front between the needles. Work the next purl stitch in the usual way.

2 When the purl stitch is complete, the yarn-over is correctly formed on the right needle with the right leg of the loop at the front of the needle.

3 On the following row, when you reach the yarn-over, knit it through the front of the loop in the usual way. This creates an open hole under the knit stitch.

Yarn-over between knit and purl stitches (Abbreviation = *yo*)

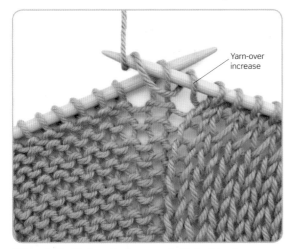

Yarn-over
increase

Yarn-over
increase

After a knit stitch and before a purl stitch: Bring the
yarn to the front between the needles, then over the top
of the right needle and to the front again. Purl the next stitch.
On the following row, work the yarn-over through the front of
the loop in the usual way to create an open hole.

After a purl stitch and before a knit stitch: Take
the yarn over the top of the right needle and to the back
of the work, then knit the next stitch. On the following row,
work the yarn-over through the front of the loop in the usual
way to create an open hole.

Yarn-over at the beginning of a row (Abbreviation = *yo*)

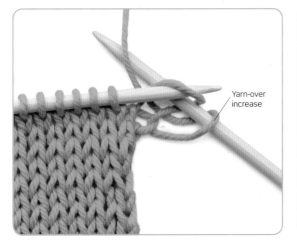

Yarn-over
increase

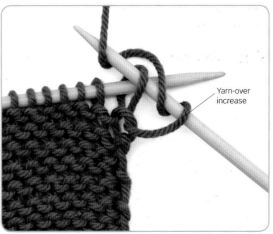

Yarn-over
increase

At the beginning of a row before a knit stitch: Insert
the tip of the right needle behind the yarn and into the first
stitch knitwise. Then take the yarn-over the top of the right
needle to the back and complete the knit stitch. On the following
row, work the yarn-over through the front of the loop in the
usual way to create an open scallop at the edge.

At the beginning of a row before a purl stitch: Wrap the
yarn from front to back over the top of the right needle
and to the front again between the needles. Then purl the
first stitch. On the following row, work the yarn-over increase
through the front of the loop in the usual way to create an
open scallop at the edge.

Simple decreases

These simple decreases are often used for shaping knitting and, paired with increases, for textured and lace stitches. More complicated decreases are always explained in knitting instructions. Most of the decreases that follow are single decreases that subtract only one stitch from the knitting, but a few double decreases are included.

Knit two together (Abbreviation = *k2tog* or *dec 1*)

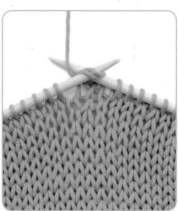

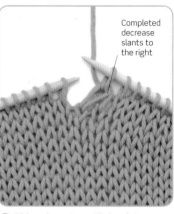

Completed decrease slants to the right

1 Insert the tip of the right needle from left to right through the second stitch then the first stitch on the left needle.

2 Wrap the yarn around the tip of the right needle, draw the yarn through both of the loops and drop the old stitches off the left needle.

3 This reduces two stitches into one and decreases one stitch in the row. The completed stitch slants to the right.

Purl two together (Abbreviation = *p2tog* or *dec 1*)

Completed decrease slants to the right on RS of work

1 Use the p2tog decrease where a pattern specifies "decrease 1" on a purl row. Insert the tip of the right needle from right to left through the first then the second stitch on the left needle.

2 Wrap the yarn around the tip of the right needle, draw the yarn through both of the loops, and drop the old stitches off the left needle.

3 This reduces two stitches into one and decreases one stitch in the row. As with the k2tog, the completed stitch slants to the right.

Slip one, knit one, pass slipped stitch over (Abbreviation = *s1 k1 psso* or *skpo*)

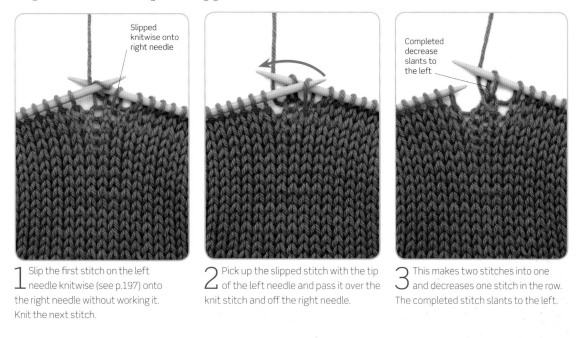

Slipped
knitwise onto
right needle

Completed
decrease
slants to
the left

1 Slip the first stitch on the left needle knitwise (see p.197) onto the right needle without working it. Knit the next stitch.

2 Pick up the slipped stitch with the tip of the left needle and pass it over the knit stitch and off the right needle.

3 This makes two stitches into one and decreases one stitch in the row. The completed stitch slants to the left.

Slip, slip, knit (Abbreviation = *ssk*)

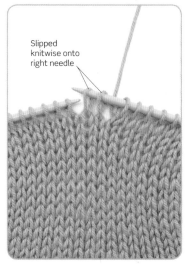

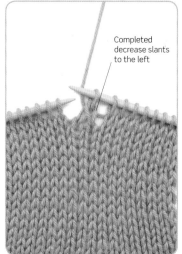

Slipped
knitwise onto
right needle

Completed
decrease slants
to the left

1 Slip the next two stitches on the left needle knitwise (see p.197), one at a time, onto the right needle without working them.

2 Insert the tip of the left needle from left to right through the fronts of the two slipped stitches (the right needle is now behind the left). Knit these two stitches together.

3 This reduces two stitches into one and decreases one stitch in the row. The completed stitch slants to the left.

Double decreases

Top stitch
in decrease
slants to
the right

Top stitch
in decrease
slants to
the left

K3tog: Insert the tip of the right needle from left to right through the third stitch on the left needle, then the second, then the first. Knit these three stitches together. This decrease loses two stitches at once.

s1 k2tog psso: Slip one stitch knitwise onto the right needle, knit the next two stitches together, then pass the slipped stitch over the k2tog and off the right needle. This decrease loses two stitches at once.

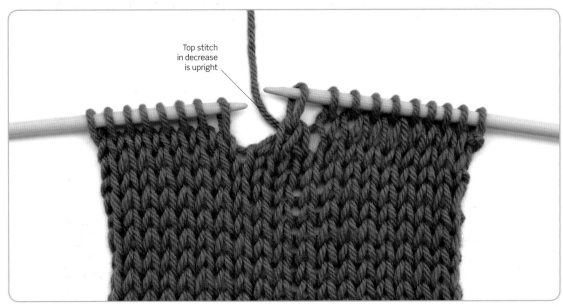

Top stitch
in decrease
is upright

s2 k1 p2sso: Slip two stitches knitwise together onto the right needle, knit the next stitch, then pass the two slipped stitches together over the knit stitch and off the right needle. This decrease loses two stitches at once.

Slip, slip, purl (Abbreviation = *ssp*)

1 Keeping yarn at the front, slip two stitches, one at a time, knitwise (see p.197) onto the right needle without working them as for ssk decrease (see p.205). Holding the needles tip to tip, insert the left needle into both stitches and transfer back to the left needle without twisting them.

2 Holding the right needle at the back, bring the tip upward from left to right through the back of the two stitches, bringing the right needle in front of the left as it comes through the stitches.

3 Lay the yarn between the needles as for purl. Take the right needle down and back through both loops, then slide them off the left needle together. This decrease loses one stitch out of the two, and so decreases one stitch.

Paired increases and decreases

Increases or decreases at each end of a row can be worked to slant left or right so that the edges mirror each other. Paired shapings should be worked at consistent intervals, and are easier if worked on a knit row. When working a pattern, one or two edge stitches can be worked plain so that the shaping does not affect the pattern.

Summary of increases and decreases

❄ PAIRED INCREASES

When made at end of a row	Abbreviation	When made at beginning of a row	Abbreviation
Slants left—increases the left edge of the knit side of stockinette stitch		**Slants right—shapes the right edge of the knit side of stockinette stitch**	
Left lifted increase	*inc1*	Right lifted increase	*inc1*
• virtually invisible • must have rows between or will pull • shows to right of increased stitch—slants the original stitch to the left and toward the selvage when used for edge shaping		• virtually invisible • must have rows between or will pull • shows to left of increased stitch—slants the original stitch to the right and toward the selvage when used for edge shaping	
Knit (or purl) in front and back of stitch	*kfb or inc1*	Knit (or purl) in front and back of stitch	*kfb or inc1*
Purl in front and back increases: • on a purl row seen from knit side, bar to the right of the stitch into which increase is made		Knit in front and back increases: • on a knit row seen from knit side, bar to the left of the stitch into which increase is made	
Make one knit (or purl) left cross	*M1k (M1p)*	Make one knit (or purl) right cross	*M1k (M1p)*
• virtually invisible • must have rows between or will pull • made between stitches, so shows where placed • slants the stitch worked after it to the left		• virtually invisible • must have rows between or will pull • made between stitches, so shows where placed • slants the stitch worked before it to the right	

❄ PAIRED DECREASES

When made at end of a row	Abbreviation	When made at start of a row	Abbreviation
Right slant—decreases the left of the knit side of stockinette stitch		**Left slant—decreases the right of the knit side of stockinette stitch**	
Knit (or purl) two together	*k2tog (p2tog)*	Slip, slip, knit (or slip, slip, purl)	*ssk (ssp)*
Knit (or purl) two together	*k2tog (p2tog)*	Slip1, knit1, pass slipped stitch over	*skp, s1 k1 psso, or skpo*
Knit (or purl) two together	*k2tog (p2tog)*	Knit (or purl) two together through back of loops	*k2tog tbl (p2tog tbl) or k-b2tog (p-b2tog)*

Paired lifted edge increase

This example increases each side of stockinette stitch using a right lifted increase (see p.199) at the start, and its paired left lifted increase at the end of every alternate knit row.

1 On an increase row, knit one stitch. Make a right lifted increase by inserting the tip of the right needle from front to back into the right side of the stitch below the next stitch on the left needle (be careful not to catch more than one strand of yarn). Knit this lifted loop.

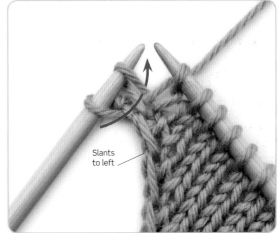

Slants to left

2 Knit to the last but one stitch of the row. Make a left lifted increase by inserting the left needle tip from front to back into the left side of the stitch two rows below the new stitch on the right needle. Knit this loop, and knit the last stitch.

3 If you find the left lifted increase awkward, pick the loop up with the left needle from back to front, slip it onto the right needle, twisting it as it is returned to the left. Knit into the front of the loop.

4 The paired increases look like this when completed over a number of rows.

Paired edge decreases (Abbreviation = *skp* and *k2tog*)

This particular example has decreases on each side of stockinette stitch. It has a slip1, knit1, pass slipped stitch over (skp) at the beginning of the row, which is paired with knit two together (k2tog) at the end of the row. Slip, slip, knit (ssk) may be substituted for skp if preferred.

1 At the start of a knit row, work a sl1, k1, psso as shown on p.205.

"k2tog" slants to the right on the left edge

"skp" slants to the left on the right edge

2 Knit to two stitches from the end of the row and knit two stitches together as shown on p.204.

Fully fashioned shaping

This method of increasing or decreasing the width of stockinette stitch preserves the line of stitches that follow the outline of the piece. Such a technique both looks attractive and makes finishing easier. Use "paired" increases and decreases on a symmetrical piece: a left slope decrease must be mirrored by a right sloping one at the other side.

On a knit row (Abbreviation = *ssk* and *k2tog*)

This example decreases one stitch at each end of a knit row but leaves two plain stitches at the selvage.

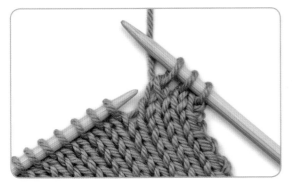

"k2tog" on stitches slanting to right on left edge

"ssk" on stitches slanting to left on right edge

1 Knit the first two stitches. Slip the next two stitches knitwise, one by one onto the right needle. Insert the left needle from left to right through the front of both stitches and knit together. This is a left-slanting ssk decrease (see p.205).

2 Knit to four stitches from the end of the row. Knit two stitches together (see p.204) and then knit the last two stitches. This decrease creates a slope to the right.

On a purl row (Abbreviation = *ssp* and *p2tog*)

This example decreases one stitch at each end of a purl row but leaves two plain stitches at the selvage.

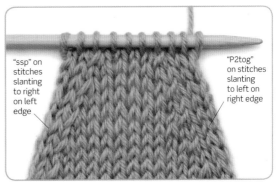

"ssp" on stitches slanting to right on left edge

"P2tog" on stitches slanting to left on right edge

1 Purl the first two stitches. Slip the next two stitches one at a time knitwise onto the right needle. Slip them back together without twisting. Insert the right needle into the front of both stitches from the right and purl them together (ssp). This decrease creates a slope to the right.

2 Work to four stitches from the end, purl two stitches together (see p.204) and purl the last two stitches. This decrease creates a slope to the left. Ssk and ssp work better than other decreases when paired with k2tog or p2tog.

Cables and twists

Many interesting textures can be created by combining knit and purl stitches in various sequences, but if you are looking for textures with higher relief and more sculptural qualities, cables and twists are the techniques to learn. Both are made by crossing stitches over each other in different ways to form an array of intricate patterns.

Simple twists

A simple twist is made over only two stitches, without a cable needle. Although twists do not create such high relief as cables, their ease and subtlety make them very popular.

The following twists are worked in stockinette stitch on a stockinette stitch ground. They can also be worked with one knit and one purl stitch—the principle is the same.

Right twist (Abbreviation = *T2R*)

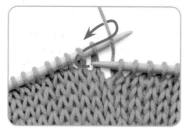 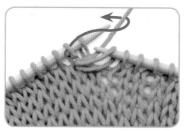 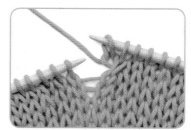

1 With yarn at the back of the right needle and in front of the left, knit the second stitch, leaving the first and second stitches on the left needle.

2 Knit the first stitch on the left needle and drop both old stitches off the left needle at the same time.

3 Without the use of a cable needle, this creates a "one-over-one" two-stitch cable slanting to the right—called a right twist.

Left twist (Abbreviation = *T2L*)

1 Insert the tip of the right needle behind the first stitch on the left needle and through the second stitch knitwise. Wrap the yarn around the right needle.

2 Pull the loop through the second stitch behind the first stitch. Be careful not to drop either the first or second stitches off the left needle yet.

3 Knit the first stitch on the left needle and drop both old stitches off the left needle. This creates a two-stitch cable slanting to the left—called a left twist.

Cables

Cables are usually worked in stockinette stitch on a reverse stockinette stitch (or garter stitch) ground. They are made by crossing two, three, four or more stitches over other stitches in the row. This technique is illustrated here with the cable 4 front and cable 4 back cables, which are crossed on every sixth row.

Cable 4 front (Abbreviation = *C4F*)

1 Work to the position of the four stockinette stitches that form the cable and slip the first two stitches onto a cable needle. With cable needle at the front, knit the next two stitches on the left needle.

2 Next, knit the two stitches from the cable needle.

3 This creates a cable crossing that slants to the left. For this reason, a "front" cable is also called a "left" cable.

Cable 4 back (Abbreviation = *C4B*)

1 Work as for Step 1 of Cable 4 front, but knit the first two stitches from the left needle with the cable needle at the back of the knitting.

2 Knit the two stitches from the cable needle.

3 This creates a cable crossing that slants to the right. For this reason, a "back" cable is also called a "right" cable.

Colorwork

The techniques for charted stockinette stitch colorwork—Fair Isle and intarsia—open up a world of richly colored designs. In Fair Isle, a yarn color is carried across the wrong side of the work until it is required. In intarsia, a separate length of yarn is used for each color and the yarns are twisted together at the color change junctures.

Following a colorwork chart

The first step in understanding charted colorwork is to grasp how to follow the charts. Rather than writing out how many stitches in which colors to work across a row, a knitting pattern provides a chart with the colors marked on it in symbols or in blocks of color. If a pattern covers the whole garment back, front, and sleeve and cannot be repeated, a large chart is provided with all the stitches on it for the entire piece. Where a pattern is a simple repeat, the repeat alone is charted. Each

square on a colorwork chart represents a stitch and each horizontal row of squares represents a row. Follow the chart from the bottom to the top, just as your knitting forms on the needles.

The chart's key tells you which color to use for each stitch. All odd-numbered rows are usually right-side (knit) rows and are read from right to left. All even-numbered rows are usually wrong-side (purl) rows and are read from left to right. Always read the instructions to ensure your chart follows these general rules.

Fair Isle chart

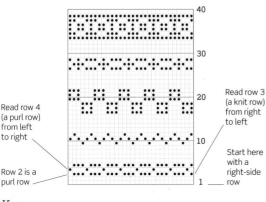

Read row 4 (a purl row) from left to right

Row 2 is a purl row

Read row 3 (a knit row) from right to left

Start here with a right-side row

Key

☐ background color
⦿ motif color

This chart example illustrates how easy it is to knit simple Fair Isle patterns. No more than two colors are used in a row, and the color not in use is "stranded" across the back until it is needed again. A chart should be worked in the Fair Isle technique if two colors are used across the entire row. If each color is used after every three or four stitches (as below), use stranding (see following page). If the colors are not used over a span of more stitches, use weaving-in (see pp.216–217). Some charts have a repeating part marked with odd stitches at each side that are worked once a row.

Intarsia chart

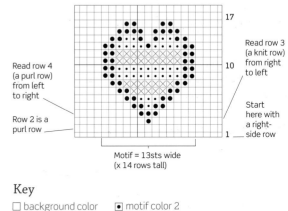

Read row 4 (a purl row) from left to right

Row 2 is a purl row

Read row 3 (a knit row) from right to left

Start here with a right-side row

Motif = 13sts wide (x 14 rows tall)

Key

☐ background color
⦿ motif color 1
⦿ motif color 2
⊠ motif color 3

This heart is an example of a simple intarsia colorwork chart. Each color on the chart is represented by a different symbol. The blank square also represents a color.

You can tell that a charted design should be worked in the intarsia technique if a color appears only in a section of a row and is not needed across the entire row. Use a separate long length of yarn, or yarn on a bobbin, for each area of color in intarsia knitting (including separated background areas). Twist the colors where they meet (see p.220).

Fair Isle method

This is where two or more colors are used in a row of knitting—traditionally, the colors would make small repeating patterns in stockinette stitch. The nonworking yarn is stranded along the wrong side, or may be woven into the back to keep it from catching.

Fair Isle stranding technique

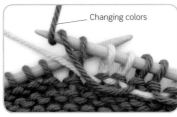

Changing colors

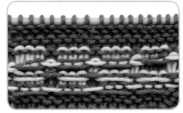

1 On the knit rows, knit the stitches in the first color, then drop it at the back and knit the stitches in the second color. Strand the color not in use loosely across the back of the work until required.

2 Work the purl rows in the same way, but strand the color not in use across the front (wrong side). Keep one color on top and the other underneath so they do not twist around each other.

3 The trick to Fair Isle knitting is to learn to keep the yarns tensioned evenly as shown here. The stranding should not be too loose or too tight. With continued practice the correct tensioning of the yarns will become automatic.

Holding the yarns

The techniques that follow for holding the yarns will speed up your work and produce more results. To maintain a consistent-weight fabric, always carry both yarns to the edge even if no stitch is required there, and twist them before starting the next row.

Holding one yarn in each hand

1 This method works well when there are only two colors in a row. Hold the first yarn over your right index finger as normal and the second over your left index finger, as shown in "Continental" style knitting (see p.176).

2 Knit the first color stitches as usual. When you reach the second color stitches keep the first color over your right index finger. Insert the right needle into the next stitch as if to knit. With your left index finger, lay the second color forward between the needles from left to right.

3 Pull the new knit loop through as usual, keeping both yarns over the correct index finger. On a purl row, follow the instructions for alternative "Continental" purl stitch (see p.176) to work the color over your left index finger.

Both yarns in right hand

Place one color over your right index finger, and one over your middle finger. Knit as normal, throwing the second color with your middle finger. This method allows you the flexibility of potentially adding a third color over your ring finger.

Both yarns in left hand

This is ideal for those who knit Continental style. Hold the first yarn over the index finger, and the second over the middle finger of your left hand. Throw the yarns with their respective finger for knit and purl as shown on p.176.

Techniques for weaving-in Fair Isle floats

When strands (or floats as they are also known) are longer than three or four stitches, they may catch on fingers or rings. To prevent this, weave the nonworking yarn into the back of the knitting by taking the weaving yarn over and under the working yarn. This can be done on every other stitch, which makes a denser fabric, or whenever a float is longer than three stitches, in which case weave into occasional stitches.

[Both hands] weaving left yarn, k or p

Weaving yarn (left)   Working yarn (right)

This method uses one yarn in each hand. Keep left yarn and finger below and to the left of needles when not weaving it in. Lift weaving yarn up, insert right needle through stitch to either knit or purl and underneath weaving yarn. Make stitch with main yarn, slipping weaving yarn over needle without catching in stitch. Knit or purl the stitch, catching floating yarn in back of the fabric. Knit the next stitch without weaving in left yarn, by dropping left finger to back so the yarn lies below the needles before making the stitch. Weave in as necessary to prevent long floats.

[Both hands] weaving right yarn, k or p

Working yarn (left)   Weaving yarn (right)

This method uses one yarn in each hand. Keep right yarn above and to the right of the needles when not weaving it in. To weave, insert right needle into stitch. Wind right yarn around needle as to knit, throw left yarn as usual to knit. Return right yarn back along its route to original position and knit the stitch. Knit the next stitch without wrapping the right yarn. Weave in as necessary to prevent long floats.

[Both hands] weaving right yarn, p

This method uses one yarn in each hand. On a purl stitch, keeping the left index finger and yarn below the needles, wind the right yarn under the right needle. Throw left yarn as usual to purl, return right yarn back along its route to original position and purl the stitch. Work the next stitch without weaving the right yarn. Weave in as necessary to prevent long floats.

Weaving index finger yarn

Holding both yarns in right hand, insert right needle into stitch, wind both yarns around needle as if to knit (or purl). Return index finger yarn back around needle to original position. Knit (or purl) the stitch with remaining yarn. Keep index finger yarn above middle finger yarn when not weaving. Knit (or purl) the next stitch without weaving the index finger yarn. Weave to prevent long floats.

[Right hand] weaving middle finger yarn, k or p

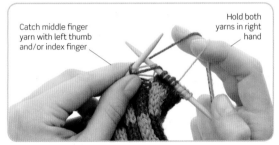

1 Hold both yarns in right hand. Keep middle finger yarn above work when not weaving in. To knit or purl, insert right needle into stitch. Bring middle finger yarn above index finger yarn, across front of both needles to the left. Holding yarn in place to the left of the needles, take it around to the right behind the needles.

2 Throw the index finger yarn as if to knit or purl, then return middle finger yarn back along its route to its original position at right back of work. Work next stitch without weaving, temporarily lowering middle finger so index finger yarn wraps around middle finger yarn. Weave in as necessary to prevent long floats.

[Left hand] weaving index finger yarn, k or p

1 Hold both yarns in left hand. Keep index finger yarn above work when not weaving in. To weave in, insert right needle into stitch making sure the needle goes over index finger yarn (drop index finger). Lay middle finger yarn over needle to work stitch as normal.

2 Draw yarn through as normal, taking care not to catch the index finger yarn into the stitch. Raise index finger yarn again and work next stitch without weaving. Weave in as necessary to prevent long floats.

[Left hand] weaving middle finger yarn, k or p

1 Here, the middle finger yarn is more awkward to weave than that on the index finger. Keep the middle finger below the work when not weaving. Insert the right needle into stitch, making sure it passes under both yarns.

2 Bring the tip back over the middle finger (weaving) yarn and catch the index finger yarn. Draw it under the middle finger yarn to make a new stitch. Work next stitch without weaving. Weave to prevent long floats.

Knit and purl Fair Isle

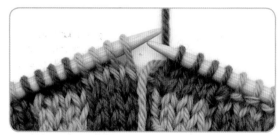

1 At the position where a purl stitch is to be introduced, bring the working yarn to the front and purl the required number of stitches. Take the yarn to the back and continue the pattern in knit stitch. Strand the yarns at the back of the knitting.

2 If you want to maintain clear color transitions, knit the first row of a new color, purl the middle rows, and knit the row immediately before a color change.

Garter stitch Fair Isle

1 Work every row of pattern twice; knit all rows. At the end of every row, wrap the yarns around each other to secure them.

2 Knit the first row (RS), stranding on the back. Start the second (WS) row with the nonworking yarn at the front and the working one at the back.

3 When it is time to change color, swap the yarn positions from front to back and continue, stranding the nonworking yarn at the front (WS) of the work.

4 For smooth transition when changing or finishing a color, do so on the first of the two-row pattern (RS) row.

Tea-cozy stitch

Wrong side of knitting

1 Twist yarns at the start of each row. Pull stranding yarn gently throughout to gather the knitting slightly. Knit 8 stitches in the first color, stranding second yarn at back. Swap yarns, knit 8 stitches in second color stranding first yarn at back. Repeat along the row.

2 Next row. First color to back, second to front, knit first 8 stitches. First color to front, second to back, knit 8 stitches in second color. Repeat along row, swapping yarns from front to back so that both yarns strand on the front. Repeat Steps 1 and 2.

Two strand laying-in

1 Work stockinette stitch in main yarn, with all yarns at back. When decorative yarns are required on knit side, bring to front between needles. Work number of stitches required in main yarn. Decorative yarns to back. Work in main yarn. Do not twist main and decorative yarns when they are moved from front to back.

2 On a purl row, all yarns to front. When decorative yarns are required to lie on the knit side, take back between needles and work number of stitches required in main yarn. Decorative yarns to front between needles. Work in main yarn.

Knit weave

1 On a K row. Both yarns at back, insert needle to knit. Lay weaving yarn right to left between needles. Knit with main yarn, do not catch weaving yarn.

2 On a P row. Both yarns at front, weaving yarn below main yarn between weaves. Insert needle to purl, lay weaving yarn right to left between needles. Purl with main yarn.

Shows on reverse of stockinette stitch. Always work one plain stitch between weaves. Twist the yarns at start of every row. Weaving yarn lies alternately over and under main yarn.

Intarsia

In the intarsia technique of colorwork, each yarn is worked separately and no strands are carried along the back (as they are in Fair Isle, see p.215). Each area of color in a row must have its own small ball of yarn. Cut short lengths from the main balls and wind onto bobbins to prevent tangles.

Intarsia technique

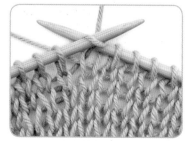

Right-slant color change: To prevent holes, twist the colors around each other only on the knit rows.

Left-slant color change: To prevent holes, twist the colors around each other only on the purl rows.

Vertical color change: To prevent holes, twist the colors around each other on both knit and purl rows.

Two-color cables

1 Wind sufficient small balls for intarsia. Work two vertical stripes of A with three-stitch vertical stripes in B and C in between (this is the six-stitch cable). Stop after the purl row before the first crossover.

2 Knit A to cable position. Slip the three C stitches off the left needle onto a cable needle and put to the back. Bring B yarn under A yarn (this is the twist) and take behind stitches on cable needle. Knit the three B stitches off the left and onto the right needle.

3 With C, and without twisting the yarn, knit the three C stitches off the cable needle and onto the right needle. Twist A under C and knit stitches between cables. On the next (purl) row, when twisting B and A the yarns will stretch diagonally at rear of crossover. Do not pull too tightly. Work seven rows of stripes to next crossover row. Work crossover as above (Steps 2–3), reversing C and B.

Colorwork stitch patterns

Slip-stitch patterns are designed specially to use more than one color in the overall pattern but only ever use one color in a row. With this technique, geometric patterns are created by working some stitches in a row and slipping others. The pattern here is shown in two different colorways and is one of the easiest to work.

Box slip-stitch pattern

Follow this pattern to work the stitch and use the steps below as a guide. Use three colors for the pattern that contrast in tone: A (a medium-toned color), B (a light-toned color), and C (a dark-toned color).

Note: Slip all slip stitches purlwise with the yarn on the WS of the work. Using A, cast on a multiple of 4 stitches, plus 2 extra.

Row 1 (WS): Using A, p to end.

Row 2 (RS): Using B, k1, s1, *k2, s2; rep from * to last 3sts, k2, s1, k1.

Row 3: Using B, p1, s1, *p2, s2; rep from * to last 3sts, p2, s1, p1.

Row 4: Using A, k to end.

Row 5: Using C, p2, *s2, p2; rep from * to end.

Row 6: Using C, k2, *s2, k2; rep from * to end.

Rep rows 1–6 to form patt.

Working a box slip-stitch pattern

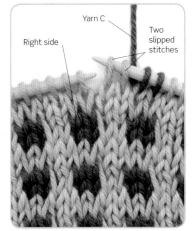

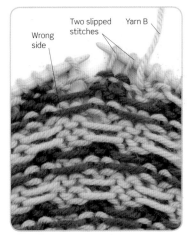

1 This shows the middle of a pattern row 6 (RS row) of the pattern above. Two stitches have been slipped. On RS rows, slip the stitches with yarn held at the back. Do not pull the yarn too tightly on the following stitches.

2 Row 4 of the pattern is worked entirely with yarn A and no stitches are slipped. The slipped stitches on the previous row and on the following row pull the stitches in A up and down to produce the box effect.

3 On WS rows of the box pattern, slip the stitches with yarn held at the front. The principle of all the slip-stitch patterns is the same—only one color is used in a row.

Short rows

Rows of knitting do not necessarily have to be knitted end to end. Short rowing, or "partial knitting," involves knitting two rows across some of the stitches, thereby adding rows in length to only one part of the fabric. It is popular for creating smooth edges in shoulder shaping, curving hems, making darts, and turning sock heels. It is most often used on stockinette stitch.

Preventing holes

In most shaping applications a concealed turn is required and there are three ways to work this: the "wrap" or "tie" (easiest and neat); the "over" (loosest); and the "catch" (neatest). Garter stitch does not require wrapping.

Wrap or tie to close holes

1 On a knit row: at turn position, slip next stitch purlwise onto right needle (see p.197), yarn to front. Return slip stitch to left needle, yarn back. Turn and purl short row. Repeat wrap at each mid-row turn.

2 On a purl row: at turn, slip next stitch purlwise, yarn to back. Slip stitch back, yarn to front. Turn and work knit short row. Repeat wrap at each mid-row turn.

3 When working across all stitches on completion of short rowing: at wrap, insert right needle up through front (knit) or back (purl) of wrap. Work wrap together with the next stitch.

Over to close holes

1 Knit or purl to turn position. Turn. Yarn to other side of work and bring yarn over needle (without moving yarn to back or front beforehand, so yarn does not go completely around needle). Work short row. When knitting across all stitches on completion of short rowing, knit yarn over and next stitch together.

2 When purling across all stitches on completion of short rowing, drop yarn over and slip next stitch purlwise. Insert left needle downward into dropped yarn, pick it up, and purl together with the next stitch.

Catch to close holes

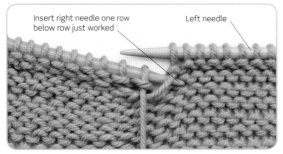

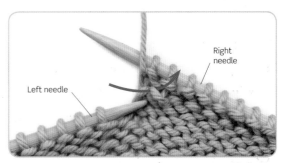

1 On either knit or purl rows, work a short row. Turn work, slip first stitch purlwise (see p.197), and work back along short row. When knitting a completion row (knitting is temporarily reversed because this makes this step easier), insert right needle down through strand between first and second stitches on left needle as shown. Lift onto left needle.

2 Turn work again and knit picked up loop together with next stitch on left needle. If completion row is purl, insert left needle upward through the strand between the first and second stitch two rows below right needle. Stretch this loop, then drop it. Slip next stitch from left to right needle. Pick up dropped loop again with the left needle. Return slipped stitch to left needle. Purl these two together.

Shaping: adapting a cast-off shoulder to short row shaping

1 This example adapts an existing left shoulder worked in stockinette stitch. The left shoulder is 24 stitches wide and the original instruction is to cast off 8 stitches every alternate row. These cast offs can be substituted by working short rows with 8 fewer stitches every alternate row. Cast on 24 stitches and work to the shoulder shaping. Ignore the cast-off instruction and knit a row.

2 Turn the work. Purl to 8 stitches from the end and work a wrap (slip next stitch purlwise, yarn back, return slip stitch, yarn forward, see opposite). Turn and knit to the end.

3 Purl to 16 stitches from the end, work wrap and turn. Knit to the end (8 stitches on needle).

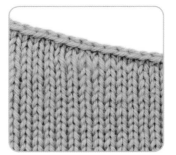

4 Purl across all the stitches, picking up wraps by slipping them onto the left needle and purling together with next stitch (opposite). Either cast off all stitches or put them onto a stitch holder for grafting later (p240).

Circular knitting

Circular knitting, or knitting in the round, is worked on a circular needle or with a set of four or five double-pointed needles. With the right side always facing, the knitting is worked around and around to form a tube, or a flat shape (a medallion). A circular needle is easy to master, while working with double-pointed needles is best suited to knitters with intermediate skills.

Knitting tubes

For those who don't enjoy stitching seams, knitting seamless tubes is a real plus. Large tubes can be worked on long circular needles, for example, for the body of a sweater or a bag.

Short circular needles are used for seamless neckbands and armhole bands, and hats. Double-pointed needles are used for smaller items, such as mittens and socks.

Working with a circular knitting needle

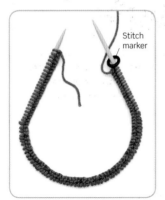

Stitch marker

1 Cast on the required number of stitches. Make sure that the stitches are untwisted and they all face inward, then slip a stitch marker onto the end of the right needle to mark the beginning of the round.

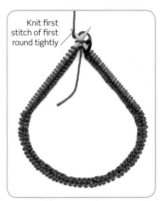

Knit first stitch of first round tightly

2 Hold the needle ends in your hands and bring the right needle up to the left needle to work the first stitch. Knit around and around on the stitches. When the stitch marker is reached, slip it from the left needle to the right needle.

3 If you are working a stockinette stitch tube on a circular needle, the right side of the work will always be facing you and every round will be a knit round.

Joining the circle of stitches

This is a neat way of closing the circle in circular knitting.

1 Cast on required number of stitches, plus one stitch. Slip the first cast-on stitch onto the right needle next to last cast-on stitch. Place the join marker after this stitch.

2 Knit the round and, when you reach the end, knit the last two stitches before the marker together (this will be the first cast-on stitch and the extra stitch).

Knitting a Mobius loop

1 Using a double cast-on (see p.182), cast on enough stitches to work a circle on a short circular needle. Knit the first round but stop before joining the circle.

2 Deliberately twist the stitches around the wire so that there is one clear twist visible, but the end stitches are facing each other with the loops facing inward.

3 Join the circle, maintaining the twist, and knit the round. The first few rounds can be tricky but once there are a few rows and the twist is established it becomes easier.

4 Continue until the loop is as deep as required. Cast off. A deep Mobius loop makes a great headband.

5 If using the Magic loop technique, moving the twist to the stitches on the right end of the needle for the first few rounds makes working them easier.

Working with a set of four double-pointed needles

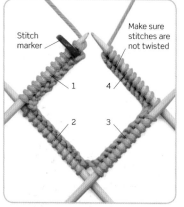

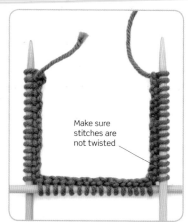

Make sure
stitches are
not twisted

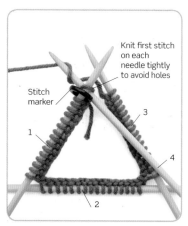

Knit first stitch
on each
needle tightly
to avoid holes

Stitch
marker

1

2

3

4

1 Your knitting instructions will specify how many double-pointed needles to use for the project you are making—either a set of four or a set of five. When working with a set of four double-pointed needles, first cast on all the stitches required to a single needle.

2 Slip some of the stitches off onto two other needles—your knitting pattern will tell you precisely how many to place on each needle. Make sure that the bottoms of the cast-on loops are all facing inward.

3 Place a stitch marker between the first and second stitches on the first needle to mark the beginning of the round. Then pull the first and third needles close together and start to knit with the fourth needle. Knit around and around in this way as for knitting with a circular needle.

Working with a set of five double-pointed needles

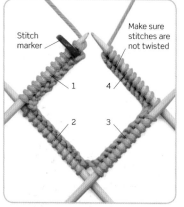

Stitch
marker

Make sure
stitches are
not twisted

1

4

2

3

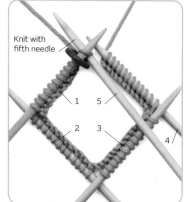

Knit with
fifth needle

1

5

2

3

4

1 Cast on, distribute the stitches and position a stitch marker as for working with four needles, but distribute the stitches over four needles.

2 Use the fifth needle to knit. Knit the first stitch tightly to close the gap between the first cast-on stitch and the last stitch.

3 When all stitches on the first needle have been knit off onto the spare needle, use this empty needle to work the stitches on the second needle. Continue around and around like this, slipping the stitch marker from the left needle to the right needle when it is reached.

Correcting mistakes

The best thing to do if you make a mistake in your knitting is to unravel it back to the mistake by unpicking the stitches one by one. If you drop a stitch, be sure to pick it up quickly before it comes undone all the way back to the cast-on edge.

Unpicking a knit row

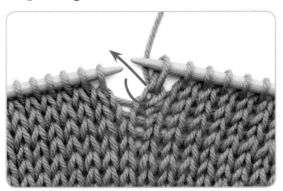

Hold the needle with the stitches in your right hand. To unpick each stitch individually, insert the tip of the left needle from front to back through the stitch below the first knit stitch on the right needle, then drop the old knit stitch off the needle and pull out the loop of yarn.

Unpicking a purl row

Hold the needle with the stitches in your right hand. Unpick each purl stitch individually with the tip of the left needle in the same way as for the knit stitch.

Picking up a dropped stitch

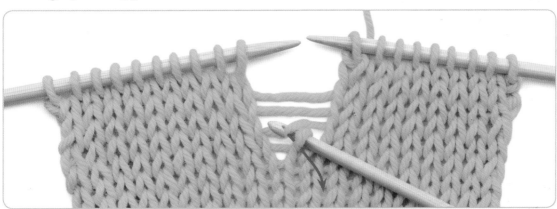

If you drop a stitch on stockinette stitch, you can easily reclaim it with a crochet hook. With the right side of the knitting facing you, insert the hook through the dropped loop. Grab the strand between the stitches and pull that strand through the loop on the hook. Continue up the rows in this way until you reach the top. Then slip the stitch back onto your needle.

Finishing details

Finishing, as its name suggests, is the final stage of a project. Details that will make your knitting easier to assemble and look more professional, such as adding borders, hems, pockets and fastenings can, with a little planning, be incorporated into the actual knitting itself.

Picking up stitches

Picking up edges is a technique that even experienced knitters can find challenging. Careful preparation and lots of practice will help. Try it out on small pieces of knitting to perfect the technique before moving on to larger or more important projects.

Cast-on/off edge

With RS facing, insert the needle in the first stitch. Leaving a long, loose end, wrap the yarn around the tip and pull it through, as if knitting a stitch. Continue, picking up and knitting one stitch through every cast-on or cast-off stitch.

Along row-ends

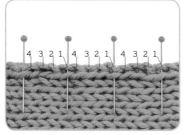

1 On lightweight or medium-weight yarn, pick up about three stitches for every four row-ends. To begin, mark out the row-ends on the right side of the knitting, placing a pin on the first of every four row-ends as shown here.

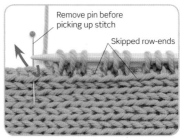

2 Pick up and knit the stitches as for picking up stitches along a cast-on edge, inserting the tip through the center of the edge stitches. Skip every fourth row-end.

With a crochet hook

1 Use a hook that fits through the stitches. With RS facing, insert the hook through the first stitch, wrap the hook behind and around the yarn from left to right and pull through.

2 Transfer the loop on the hook onto a needle. Pull yarn to tighten. Repeat, transferring the loops to the needle.

Tips for picking up stitches

A yarn in a contrasting color is used in the step-by-step instructions for picking up stitches to clearly illustrate the process. You can hide picking-up imperfections, however, if you use a matching yarn. For a contrasting border, switch to the new color on the first row of the border.

Always pick up and knit stitches with the right side of the knitting facing you, since picking up stitches creates a ridge on the wrong side of the work.

Your knitting pattern will most likely specify which needle size to use for picking up stitches—usually one size smaller than the size used for the main knitting.

After you have picked up the required number of stitches, work the border following the directions given in your pattern, whether it is ribbing, seed stitch, garter stitch, or a fold-over hem.

It is difficult to pick up stitches "evenly" along an edge. To help get the most even pickup, try casting the work off again, either looser or tighter. If this doesn't work, pull out the border and try again, adjusting the number of stitches or spreading them out in a different way. Alternatively, try a smaller needle size if the border looks too stretched, or a larger needle size if it looks too tight.

Along a curved edge

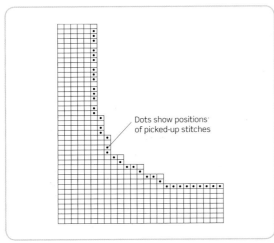

Dots show positions of picked-up stitches

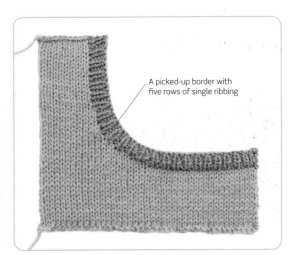

A picked-up border with five rows of single ribbing

1 When working picked-up armhole borders or neckbands, you will be required to pick up stitches along a curved edge. As a general rule, you can follow this diagram when picking up stitches along a curved edge. Pick up one stitch in each cast-off stitch and three stitches for every four row-ends. Along the actual curve, ignore the corner stitches along the stepped decreases to smooth out the curve.

2 Once all the stitches have been picked up, work the border as instructed in your knitting pattern.

Selvages

The selvage can make all the difference to a free edge and there are many methods that are decorative as well as functional. Loose edges can be tightened with chain or slipped garter, and rolling edges controlled with a garter selvage. Both selvages do not have to be worked the same.

Garter selvage

1 This is best for edges that will not be sewn together because it can make a bumpy seam. It encourages the edge of stockinette stitch to lie flat. Each "bump" equals two rows.

2 On stockinette stitch, knit the first and last stitch of every row.

Slipped garter selvage

Firmer than garter selvage.

1 Slip first stitch knitwise and knit last stitch on all rows.

2 The resulting edge is firmer than garter selvage, and smoother. The slipped stitches can aid picking up on some projects.

Double slipped garter selvage

Good for slightly decorative free edges.

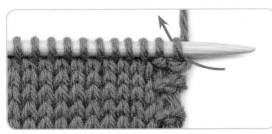

1 Work all rows the same. Insert the right needle into the back of the first stitch from right to left and slip the stitch.

2 Knit the second stitch. Work as pattern to two from end of the row and then knit the last two stitches.

Chain selvage

Best for picking up stitches into (see pp.228–229), crochet edgings, and backstitch (but not mattress stitch) seams (see p.241).

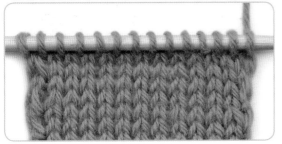

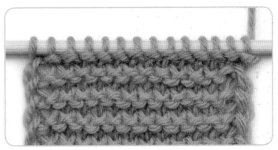

1 On stockinette stitch, all right-side rows slip first stitch knitwise, and knit last stitch. On all wrong-side rows, slip first stitch purlwise, and purl last stitch.

2 On garter stitch, with yarn in front slip first stitch purlwise, yarn back and knit to the end.

Picot loop selvage

1 Right-side rows, insert right needle knitwise into first two stitches, bring yarn around front of right needle from left to right and work a yarn-over (see p.202) while knitting first two stitches together. Knit to last two stitches, slip them knitwise one by one, and insert left needle into front to make an ssk decrease (see p.205).

2 Wrong-side rows, loosely work a purl yarn-over (see p.202, hold it open with your thumb if necessary), and purl rest of row. On garter stitch, purl first and last two stitches.

Eyelets and buttonholes

The simplest form of buttonhole is an eyelet, but there are techniques for larger, stronger ones that will take different-sized buttons. Although horizontal buttonholes are the most common, vertical and diagonal variations are also included in this section.

Open eyelet

1 For an open eyelet on a stockinette stitch ground, work a yarn-over on the right needle (see p.202). Then work a "s1 k1 psso" decrease (see p.205) after the yarn-over.

2 The yarn-over creates a hole and the decrease compensates for the extra loop, so that the knitting remains the same width.

3 On the following row, purl the yarn-over in the usual way. Open eyelets can be arranged in various ways to create any number of different lace textures.

Positioning buttons and buttonholes

Decide on the number of buttons before knitting the buttonholes. Work holes to match the button size. Top and bottom buttons are usually positioned between ½in (1cm) and 1¼in (3cm) from neck and hem edges. Start buttonholes at least three stitches from the edge. Count rows and stitches, as measuring may be inaccurate. For vertically worked bands, knit and attach the buttonband first. Mark the top and bottom button positions with thread.

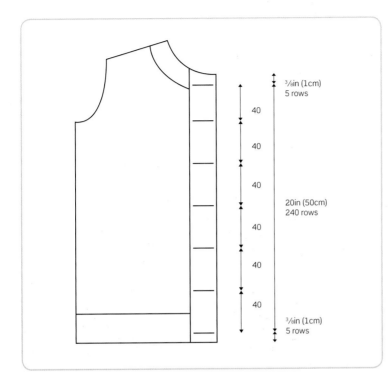

³⁄₈in (1cm)
5 rows

40

40

40

20in (50cm)
240 rows

40

40

40

³⁄₈in (1cm)
5 rows

1 Knit the buttonhole band, working the calculated number of rows between buttonholes, allowing two rows for a two-row buttonhole. Work vertical buttonhole rows so that they center on the marker.

2 For a horizontally worked picked-up buttonband, count stitches rather than rows to calculate the spacing as described in Step 1.

Altering patterns

You can alter the length of garment patterns worked in plain garter or stockinette stitch, but avoid altering armholes, necklines, or sleeve heads. Since sleeves and some bodies have shaping, this must also be adjusted. Make notes at every step. In this example, length is being added to a sleeve:

1 Copy, photocopy, or draw out the pattern diagram. Write the new required length on the diagram (e.g., 20in).
2 Find the number of rows to 4in in the gauge note. Divide that number by 10 to calculate how many rows there are in 1in. For example, 32 rows per 4in. 32 ÷ 4 = 8 rows per 1in.
3 Multiply the required new length by the number of rows in 1in. The resulting figure is the total number in the new length. For example, 20 × 8 = 160 rows.
4 Any increasing will also have to be recalculated. From the pattern, note the number of stitches to cast on at the cuff and how many there will be on the needle just before the start of the underarm shaping (this figure should be shown at the end of the written instruction for the increases).

5 Subtract the smallest from the largest amount of stitches. The answer is the total number of stitches to be increased. Divide the answer by two (because a sleeve has two sides), to give the number of stitches to increase on each side. For example: 114 – 60 = 54 sts. 54 ÷ 2 = 27 sts.
6 To calculate the number of rows between each increase, divide the new number of rows found in Step 3 by the number of increases calculated in Step 5. If you have a fraction in this answer, round the number down. For example, 144 ÷ 27 = 4.22. Increase one stitch each side every four rows. Knit the remainder of the rows even before doing the underarm cast-offs.

Reinforced eyelet buttonhole

1 On a knit row, work to position of buttonhole. Make a yarn-over (see p.202). Work to end of row. On next row, slip the yarn-over purlwise and make another front-to-back yarn-over. Work to the end of the row.

2 On the next row, slip the stitch before the yarn-overs knitwise. Knit both yarn-overs together but do not drop from the left needle.

3 Pass the slipped stitch over the newly made stitch. Knit three stitches together (the yarn-overs and the following stitch). Work to the end of the row.

4 This buttonhole is stronger and neater than a simple open eyelet buttonhole (see p.232).

One-row horizontal buttonhole

This strong buttonhole is worked on stockinette stitch in this example, but looks particularly neat on a garter stitch or reverse stockinette stitch project.

1 Work to buttonhole position (this should be a knit row on reverse stockinette stitch). Yarn to front. Slip one stitch purlwise. Yarn back.

2 Slip one stitch purlwise and pass previous stitch over. Repeat this step across the number of buttonhole stitches required.

3 Slip the last stitch on right needle back to the left. Turn work. Yarn back. Cast on the number of stitches for the buttonhole using cable cast-on (see p.180). Cast on one more stitch, bring yarn forward after making stitch but before placing it on the left needle. Turn work.

4 Slip one stitch knitwise and pass the last cast-on stitch over it. Work the rest of the row.

5 This buttonhole is worked the same on reverse stockinette stitch.

Vertical buttonhole

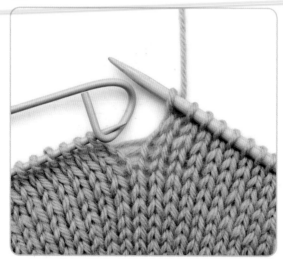

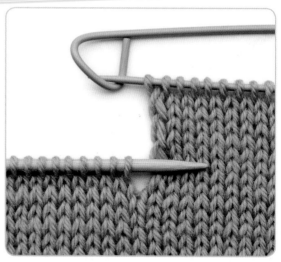

1 This example is in stockinette stitch. Work to the position of the buttonhole. Slip the stitches that will be to the left of the buttonhole onto a stitch holder. Turn work. Work right side of buttonhole starting with a purl row, making a chain selvage (see p.231) by slipping first edge stitch purlwise on all wrong-side rows, and knitting last edge stitch on all right-side rows.

2 Once the right side is long enough, finish on a purl row, break the yarn leaving a long tail, and slip right-side stitches onto another holder. Slip held stitches back onto the left needle with right side facing. Join in the new end of yarn (leaving a long tail) and make a right lifted increase (see p.200) between the first and the second stitches.

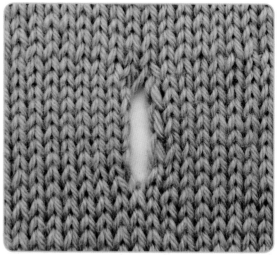

3 Slip the last stitch knitwise on the next and all wrong-side rows and knit it into the back of the first stitch on all right-side rows. This creates a variation of a chain selvage (see p.231) on the left side of the buttonhole.

4 When both sides have equal rows, making sure you finish on a purl row, break the yarn leaving a long tail, and restore all stitches to the needles in the correct order. Join the yarn in and work a complete row, working the two selvage stitches of the buttonhole together. Weave in ends neatly.

Diagonal buttonhole

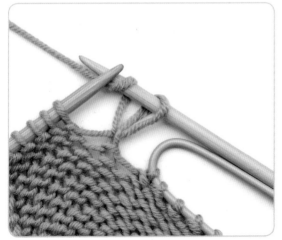

1 Working in stockinette stitch, knit to the position of the buttonhole. Slip the stitches that will be to the left of the buttonhole onto a stitch holder. Turn the work. Slip the first stitch purlwise. Make a yarn-over. Purl to the end.

2 Knit the next row to yarn-over, and knit into the back of the yarn-over, twisting it to close the hole. Knit the last stitch. Repeat for the required length of the buttonhole, ending with a purl row. Repeat knit instruction in Step 1.

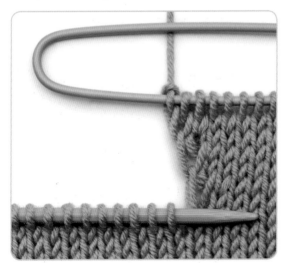

3 Break the yarn, leaving a long tail and slip right-side stitches onto another holder. Slip held stitches back onto the left needle with right side facing. Join in new end of yarn and make a right lifted increase (see p.200) between first and second stitches.

4 Knit into the back of the first stitch and knit to the end. Purl the next row to three stitches from the end. Purl the next two stitches together and slip the last stitch knitwise. Repeat for the required length of buttonhole, ending with a purl row.

5 Break the yarn, leaving a long tail and restore all stitches to needles in the correct order. Join in the yarn and work a complete row, working the two selvage stitches of the buttonhole together. Weave in ends neatly. To slant the buttonhole the other way, reverse the increase and decrease.

Blocking

Always refer to your yarn label or ballband before blocking. Textured stitch patterns, such as garter stitch, ribbing, and cables, are best wet blocked or steamed extremely gently so that their texture is not altered—they should never be pressed or stretched.

Wet blocking

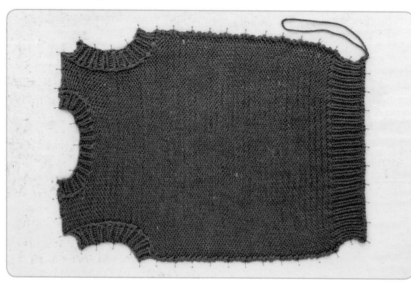

If your yarn allows, wet blocking is the best way to even out your knitting. Using lukewarm water, either wash the piece or simply wet it. Squeeze and lay it flat on a towel, then roll the towel to squeeze out more moisture. Pin the piece into shape on layers of dry towels covered with a sheet. Let dry.

Steam blocking

Only steam block if your yarn allows. Pin the piece to the correct shape, then place a clean damp cloth on top. Use a warm iron to create steam, barely touching the cloth. Do not rest the iron on the knitting, and avoid any garter stitch or ribbed areas. Before removing the pins, let the piece dry completely.

Seams

The most popular seam techniques for knitting are mattress stitch, edge-to-edge stitch, backstitch, and whipstitch. Cast-off and grafted seams are sometimes called for and learning to graft open stitches together for a seamless join is very useful.

Figure-eight start for seams

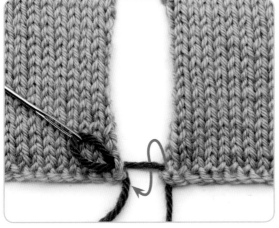

1 Lay pieces to be joined side by side, right sides facing you. Thread the needle and bring it from back to front through the bottom stitch of the right piece. Take the needle under the left piece and insert it back to front through the bottom stitch.

2 Take the needle to the right piece and bring it from back to front through the bottom stitch again. This makes a figure of eight—a strong, neat start to a seam.

Mattress stitch

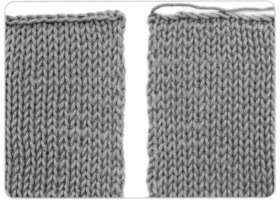

1 Mattress stitch is nearly invisible and is the best seam technique for ribbing and stockinette stitch. Start by aligning the edges of the pieces to be seamed with both the right sides facing you.

2 Insert the needle from the front through the center of first knit stitch on one piece of knitting and up through the center of stitch two rows above. Repeat on the other piece, working up the seam and pulling edges together.

Edge-to-edge seam

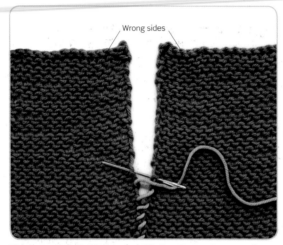

Wrong sides

This seam is suitable for most stitch patterns. To start, align the pieces of knitting with the wrong sides facing you. Work each stitch of the seam through the little bumps formed along the edges of knitting as shown.

Whipstitch seam

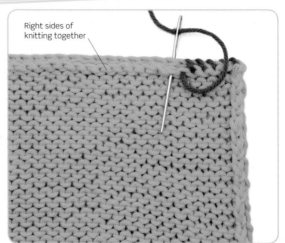

Right sides of knitting together

This seam is also called an oversewn seam or an overcast stitch seam. With the right sides together, insert the needle from back to front through both layers, working through the centers of the edge stitches (not through the bumps this time). Make each stitch in the same way.

Grafted seam

This seam can be worked along two pieces of knitting that have not been cast off or along two cast-off edges as shown here; the principle for both is the same.

1 With the right sides facing you, follow the path of a row of knitting along the seam as shown.

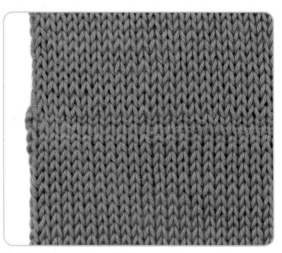

2 When the seam is grafted in a matching yarn as here, the seam blends in completely and makes it look like one continuous piece of knitting.

Backstitch seam

Backstitch can be used for almost any seam on knitting, but is not suitable for super-bulky yarns. To start, align the pieces of knitting with the right sides together. Make one stitch forward and then one stitch back into the starting point of the previous stitch, as shown. Work the stitches as close to the edge of the knitting as possible.

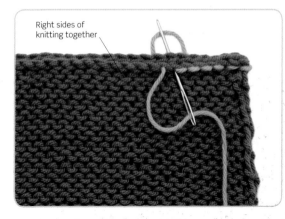

Right sides of knitting together

Picot hem

1 Using smaller needles, cast on an even number of stitches to the length of the hem using backward loop cast-on (see p.178). Work the required depth of hem in stockinette stitch, ending with a purl row. Next row, knit first two stitches together (see p.204), make a yarn-over by bringing yarn forward and back over the needle (see p.202). Repeat to the end of the row.

Yarn over lace holes

2 Now, change to larger needles. Knit stitches and yarn-overs on the first row, work an equal depth of hem in stockinette stitch, ending on a purl row.

3 When the piece is completed, fold the hem up at lace holes with wrong sides together. Pin so that the stitches are in line. Working from the wrong side, whipstitch in place along a row using hem yarn and a darning needle as follows: insert needle into a reverse stitch loop and then its vertically matching cast-on loop, pull yarn through and repeat.

4 Do not allow the sewing to pucker the knitting. Block the hem (see p.238) with the garment to achieve the final effect.

Sewing on an edging

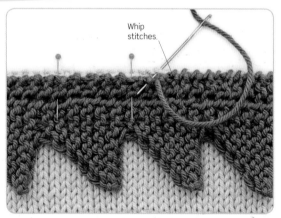

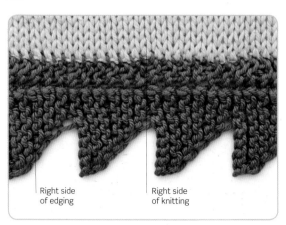

Right side
of edging

Right side
of knitting

1 Sew the edges together with even, closely worked whipstitches.

2 Open out the finished seam and steam very lightly if the yarn allows it (see p.238).

Fastenings

Choose an appropriate size and material for your project. Although nylon and plastic fastenings are lighter and less obtrusive, metallic or contrasting colored ones can make a statement. Riveted snaps can be used; insert the shank between stitches, and when connecting top to bottom, make sure there are no sharp edges to cut stitches.

Attaching snaps

The male side of the snap goes on the inside of the outer layers of a garment. Decide position of snaps. Measuring can be inaccurate; count exact stitches and rows on each piece and mark positions with a contrasting thread.

1 Make a knot and sew in the end of the thread at the marker, catching only half of each strand of yarn so that stitches don't go through to right side. Place snap in position centrally over the marker and insert the needle inward through the surface of the yarn near a stud hole just below the snap edge, then bring it up through the snap hole.

2 Repeat this three or four times through each hole, never taking the needle through to the right side. Move the needle to the next hole and repeat. To secure the thread, sew two small backstitches, then sew a loop, thread the needle back through, and pull tightly.

Sewing in a zipper

1 Match the color and the weight of zipper to the yarn, and be sure to knit the length of the garment to match zipper lengths available. Work a garter selvage (see p.230) at the zipper edge.

2 Close the zipper. With right sides facing, pin the top and bottom of knitting to the zipper first, making sure the teeth are covered by the knitted edge. Pin the center, then the centers of the remaining sections, easing the rows so they are evenly distributed. Pin horizontally rather than vertically. Do one side at a time and be sure to use plenty of pins.

3 Baste the zipper in place with contrasting sewing thread, sewing between the same vertical lines of stitches. With a sharp daring needle and knitting yarn (or matching sewing thread), backstitch neatly upward from the hem, sewing between the same vertical lines of stitches.

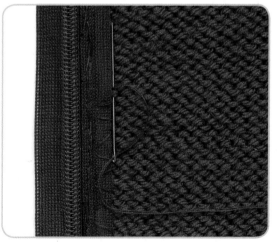

4 Turn the garment inside out. With knitting yarn, or matching sewing thread, slip stitch the outer edges of the zipper to the knitting, sewing into the back of the same vertical lines of stitches.

Embellishments

Plain knitting sometimes calls out for a little embellishment. Whether it's adding pom-poms to a hat, threading tassels onto the ends of a scarf, or highlighting a motif with decorative embroidery, here are some techniques to give your projects that perfect finishing touch.

Pom-poms

1 Draw two 3¼in (8cm) diameter circles on cardboard. Draw another 1in (2.5cm) diameter circle in the centers. The diameter of the outer circle minus that of the inner will be the approximate size of the pom-pom. A smaller center circle makes a denser pom-pom. Cut out circles and centers so they look like doughnuts. Cut a few 1yd (1m) lengths of yarn and wind together into a small ball. Put the circles together. Hold the yarn ends at the edge of the circle and push the ball through the center, winding the yarn through the circles. Continue winding.

2 When the first ball runs out, make another. If the center becomes too tight, thread as many strands of yarn as possible onto a darning needle, and use this to complete the winding. Insert the point of scissors into the outside of the circle and cut through the wraps.

3 Slide a long doubled strand of yarn between the circles, wrap and knot it tightly around the core.

4 Thread the yarn onto a needle and make a few stitches through the knot. Gently remove the circles. Shake and trim the pom-pom, but do not cut the tie strands. Suspending a wool pom-pom in steam will make it even fuller (hang it at the end of a long needle for safety).

Tassels

1 Select a template approximately the length of the finished tassel; this can be cut cardboard, but a book is often ideal. Holding the end with your thumb, wrap the yarn repeatedly around the template using single or varied colors. Fifty wraps is average; more wraps make a thicker tassel. With a threaded needle, pull a long doubled strand of yarn between the yarn and the template, and slide it up to the end. Tie it tightly around the strands, leaving long ends.

2 Insert scissors at the base of the wraps and cut across all strands. Remove the template.

3 Wrap another strand of yarn tightly around the top a short distance below the head, then tie securely and sew the ends through the wraps and into the tassel head a few times.

4 Trim the ends of the tassel and sew to your project with the remaining long strand at the head. Light pressing or steaming at the end of Step 2 makes the tassel sleeker.

Fringe

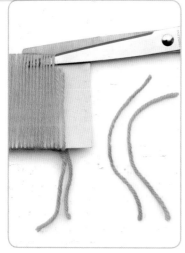

1 Cut a cardboard template a little wider than the fringe length required. Wind the yarn repeatedly around the cardboard. Cut along one side of the cardboard, making lengths of yarn double the width of the cardboard.

2 Take several lengths (more make a thicker fringe), fold in half, and hold the folded loop in front of the fabric edge. Insert a crochet hook through the back of specially made selvage holes. Catch the folded loop and pull it through to the back.

3 Catch the strands in the hook again and pull through the first loop. Repeat along the edge, spacing as required. Trim the ends evenly. Fringes can be beaded, knotted, or worked in silky or contrasting colored yarns.

Running stitch

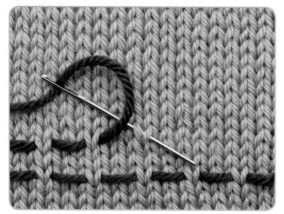

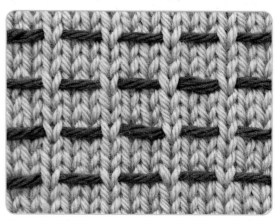

1 Secure the yarn on the wrong side of the work. Bring the needle through to the front between two stitches at the end of the line to be worked. Then, take the needle to the back between two stitches a measured number of stitches or rows to the right (or left).

2 Repeat, spacing the stitches in an even pattern as required, being careful not to pucker the fabric.

Bullion stitch

To begin the stitch, secure the yarn on the wrong side and bring the needle through to the right side at one end of the position for the stitch. Then insert the needle through to the back a short distance from the starting point and out to the front again at the starting point. Wrap the yarn at least six times around the needle close to the knitting and, holding the wraps with your fingers, pull the needle carefully through the wraps. To complete the stitch, reinsert the needle through the knitting at the same place (as shown by the arrow). Arrange the bullion stitches in spirals to form rose shapes, or as here to form simple star or flower-petal shapes.

Lazy daisy stitch

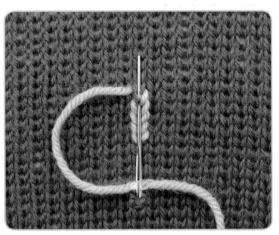

Lazy daisy stitches are individual chain stitches held down at the loop end by a short stitch. They are traditionally used to form flower shapes. To begin the stitch, secure the yarn on the wrong side and bring the needle through at the center of the flower. Reinsert the needle through to the back at the starting point and bring it out to the front a short distance away as shown. Secure the loop with a short stitch. Work all the "petals" in the same way, starting each one at the flower center.

Duplicate stitch worked vertically

1 Secure the embroidery yarn on the wrong side of the stockinette stitch, then pass the needle from back to front through the center of a knit stitch and pull the yarn through. Next, insert the needle from right to left behind the knit stitch above, as shown, and pull the yarn through.

2 Insert the needle from front to back and to front again under the top of the stitch below, so it comes out in the center of the stitch just covered, as shown. Continue in this way, tracing the path of the knitting vertically.

Glossary

backstitch A sewing stitch used for a firm, straight seam that is worked from the wrong side.

ballband The wrapper around a ball of yarn that usually details fiber content, weight, length, needle size, gauge, and cleaning instructions.

bias knitting Diagonally shaped pieces of knitting that slope to the left or right.

blocking The finishing process for a piece of knitting in which it is set in shape using water or steam.

bulky yarn Also called super bulky, roving, or 16-ply (and upward) (yarn symbol 6). A bulky yarn is suitable for heavy blankets, rugs, and thick scarves.

cable A design made by crossing one or more stitches over other stitches in a row; frequently resembles a rope or cable. Twist stitches belong to the same family.

cable cast-on A method of casting on that produces firm, cordlike knitting that holds a neat and defined edge.

cable needle A short double-ended needle, often with a bend in the middle, that is used to hold the slipped stitches while working cables.

carrying up the side A method for keeping the edges of a two-colored, even-row stripe pattern neat. The yarns are twisted around each other and carried up the side of the piece.

cast off in pattern Cast off while working stitches used in the previous row.

cast off in ribbing Cast off while working stitches in the ribbing used in the previous row.

casting off/binding off Completing a piece of knitting by finishing off the loops of the stitches so that they cannot unravel.

casting off knitwise/purlwise Cast off while working the stitches in knit/purl.

casting on Forming an initial number of stitches on a needle at the start of a piece of knitting. There are various methods, depending on the effect you want to achieve.

chunky yarn Also called super chunky, 14-ply, craft, or rug (yarn symbol 5). A chunky yarn is suitable for rugs, jackets, blankets, hats, leg warmers, and other winter accessories.

circular knitting Working on circular needles or double-pointed needles to produce a seamless item such as a hat or socks. There is no need to turn the work and no wrong-side row. Sometimes called tubular knitting.

circular needles A pair of needles connected by a flexible wire, usually used for circular knitting and very wide projects that cannot fit on conventional straight needles.

colorwork Any method of incorporating color into your knitting. This includes stripes, Fair Isle, intarsia, and slipped stitch patterns.

decreases/decreasing Techniques that subtract stitches. Used to shape knitting and to form textures in combination with other stitches.

double-knit yarn (DK) A medium-weight yarn. Also called 5–6-ply or light worsted (yarn symbol 3). A light yarn for sweaters, lightweight scarves, blankets, and toys.

double-pointed needles Knitting needles with a tip at each end; a set of four or five is used for the circular knitting of small items, such as mittens and socks.

Fair Isle A method in which two different colored yarns are worked across a row and any yarn color not being worked is carried across the back of the work (also known as stranded) until required. This unworked yarn can also be woven in.

fibers Yarn is made up of fibers, such as the hair from an animal, man-made (synthetic) fibers, or fibers derived from a plant. The fibers are processed and spun into yarn.

fine yarn Also called 4-ply, sport, or baby (yarn symbol 2). A fine yarn suitable for lightweight sweaters, babywear, socks, and accessories.

fingering yarn Also called 2-ply or lace (yarn symbol 0). A very fine yarn for knitting lace.

fully fashioned shaping An attractive method for increasing and decreasing when working stockinette stitch, in which a line of stitches is preserved to follow the edge of the piece.

garter stitch Working in knit stitches on every row, whichever side of the knitting is facing you. It produces a thick fabric, which is identical on both sides and will not curl at the edges.

gauge The size of the stitches in a piece of knitting (UK: tension), measured by the number of stitches and rows to 4in (10cm), or to 1in (2.5cm) on fine knitting.

gauge swatch A square knitted to the required number of stitches and rows to match the stated gauge of a project, usually 4in (10cm) square. A knitter must achieve the gauge stated in a pattern, or else the knitted item will not end up the correct size.

I-cord A narrow tube of knitting, created on a knitting dolly or cord-maker, or knitted on double-pointed needles. Used as cords, straps, ties, or as a trimming.

increases/increasing Created stitches during knitting. Can be combined with other stitches in order to form shapes and textures.

intarsia A method for working with different colored yarns to create blocks of color. A separate length of yarn is used for each color of the motif and twisted where the color changes to prevent holes; yarns are not stranded across the reverse of the work. Uses less yarn than Fair Isle knitting.

knit-on cast-on This cast-on uses two needles to combine a cast-on with the knitting of the first row. If worked through the front of the loops, it produces a soft edge; if through the back of the loops, the edge is firmer.

knit stitch One of two basic stitches used to form knitting.

knitting through back of loop Stitches that twist the stitch in the row below

so that the legs of the stitch cross at the base.

knitwise Working with knit stitches facing you, insert the right-hand needle into a stitch as if to knit it.

live stitches Stitches that are currently being worked.

mattress stitch A seaming stitch, which is almost invisible, used to sew pieces of knitting together with the right sides facing. It forms only a small seam on the wrong side of the work.

pick up and knit Draw loops through the edge of the knitting and place them on the needle.

picot A looped or scalloped effect along an edge, may be decorative or functional.

pilling When the surface of a knitted item rubs up into tiny balls, due to wear and friction.

plied yarn A yarn made from more than one strand of spun fiber, so 4-ply yarn is four strands plied together. Most knitting yarns are plied, since plying prevents the yarn from twisting and resulting fabric slanting diagonally.

pom-pom A small, fluffy ball made of yarn, used as trimming or decoration.

purl stitch One of two basic stitches used to form knitting.

purlwise Working stitches facing you, inserting the right-hand needle into a stitch as if to purl it.

ribbing/rib/rib stitch Knitting with great elasticity, used where fabric needs to hold tightly to the body, but is capable of expanding. Single ribbing or 1x1 rib is knit 1, purl 1; 2x2 rib is knit 2, purl 2; 3x3 rib is knit 3, purl 3.

selvage The integral edge of the fabric; in simple stockinette or garter stitch, this is formed by the last stitch of one row and the first stitch of the following row.

short-row shaping Used for shaping shoulders, curving hems, making darts, and turning sock heels. Rows are added in only one part of the fabric by knitting part of a row instead of knitting it to the end. It uses one of three turning methods to close up holes.

slipknot A knot that you form when you place the first loop on the needle as you start casting on stitches.

slip stitch Sliding a stitch from the left-hand needle to the right-hand needle without working it. The usual method is to slip the stitches purlwise; less frequently, stitches are slipped knitwise. Slipped stitches at the beginning of each row—slipped selvages—can help to create a very neat edge.

stitch holder Often shaped like a large safety pin, stitches can be slipped onto this to prevent them from dropping while other stitches in the row are worked, or to be held until cast off later.

stitch marker Something used to mark a significant position in a row of knitting, commercially available as closed or split versions, but can be homemade from scraps of yarn.

stockinette stitch A stitch formed by knitting all stitches when the right side of the work is facing you, and purling all stitches when the wrong side of the work is facing you. stockinette stitch knitting curls at the edges of the fabric.

stranding Laying yarns straight along the wrong side of knitting, commonly referred to in Fair Isle knitting, the strands created are sometimes called "floats."

superfine yarn Also called 3-ply, fingering or baby (yarn symbol 1). A very fine yarn suitable for fine-knit socks, shawls, and babywear.

three-needle cast-off/bind-off Casting-off method that binds two sets of stitches together, while casting off simultaneously. This creates a firm, neat seam, with a smooth finish on the right side of the work. It is a good way of finishing the toe of a sock or the fingertip area of a mitten.

twist Two stitches twisted together to form a narrow cable, which slants left or right. A cable needle is not used.

weaving in ends The process of completing a piece of knitting by sewing yarn ends (such as from the cast-on or cast-off edges or the ends of balls of yarn) into the knitting to disguise them.

whipstitch Stitch used to seam two pieces of knitting by placing them right sides together and then sewing through the edge stitches. Also called overcast.

work even Work in the specified pattern without increasing or decreasing.

worsted yarn Also called medium, 12-ply, aran, or Afghan (yarn symbol 4). A medium yarn suitable for sweaters, blankets, hats, scarves, and mittens.

yarn Fibers that have been spun into a long strand to be used in knitting. Yarns may be made of natural fibers, a blend of two, or even non-standard materials.

yarn bobbins Small plastic shapes for holding yarn when doing intarsia work, where there are many yarns in different colors.

yarn over An instruction to increase by adding stitches and creating holes at the same time. Yarn-overs (yo) are used for decorative purposes, such as producing lacy knitting. There are various types: yarn-over between knit stitches; yarn-over between purl stitches; yarn-over between knit and purl stitches; and yarn-over at the beginning of a row.

Index

A

abbreviations 195
acrylic yarns 155
Afghan yarns 164
alt 195
altering patterns 233
alternating-loop cast-on 181
Aran yarns 164, 165

B

baby patterns
  baby booties 30–31
  baby Fair Isle cardigan 14–19
  baby mittens 36–37
  baby pom-pom hat 12–13
  circles crib blanket 26–29
  simple baby beanie hat 10–11
back of loop, knitting through 197
backstitch seam 241
ballbands 163
balls of yarn 162
  joining on a new ball 185
bamboo needles 168
beanie hat 122–123
beg 195
blankets
  chunky cable lap blanket 130–131
  circles crib blanket 26–29
  patchwork blanket 132–137
blocking 238
  steam blocking 238
  wet blocking 238
blunt-ended yarn needles 186
bobbins 162
boot cuffs 110–111
booties, baby 30–31
bouclé yarns 159
braided yarns 157
bulky yarns 164, 165
bullion stitch 247
buttonholes
  diagonal buttonhole 237
  one-row horizontal buttonhole 235
  positioning 232–233
  reinforced eyelet buttonhole 234
  vertical buttonhole 236
buying yarn 162

C

cable cast-on 180
cable needles 168
cables 213
  baby pom-pom hat 12–13
  boot cuffs 110–111
  cable 4 back 213
  cable 4 front 213
  cable and bobble sweater 86–89
  cabled bobble hat 96–97
  cabled pillow cover 144–145
  cabled scarf 124–125
  chunky cable lap blanket 130–131
  ear warmer headband 76–77
  short cabled socks 106–109
  slouchy hat 98–99
  textured sweater 114–117
  wrist warmers 100–101
cast-offs 186–189, 195
  cast off in pattern 195
  casting off in rib effect 187
  casting off knitwise 186
  chain cast-off 186
  crochet cast-off 188
  decrease cast-off 189
  delayed cast-off 188
  purl cast-off 187
  slipping stitches off the needle 186
  suspended cast-off 188
  three-needle cast-off 189
cast-ons 178–185, 195
  alternating-loop cast-on 181
  cable cast-on 180
  contrast-edge cast-on 183
  double cast-on 182
  double-twist-loop cast-on 181
  finger loop cast-on 180
  invisible cast-on 185
  knit-on cast-on 179
  knit-stitch cast-on 179
  long-tail cast-on 182
  single cast-on 178
  single strand cast-ons 178–185
  thumb cast-on 178
  tubular cast-on 185
  twisted long-tail cast-on 184
chain cast-off 186
chain selvage 231
charts
  colorwork 214
  Fair Isle 214
  intarsia 214
  stitch symbols 194
check slip-stitch patterns 221
chenille yarns 156
children's patterns
  child's beanie hat 54–55
  child's cowl hood 60–61
  child's easy mittens 74–75
  child's hat with ear flaps 62–63
  child's striped scarf 56–59
  color block sweater 44–47
  Fair Isle sweater dress 48–51
  hooded scarf 70–73
  Norwegian sweater 40–43
  sheep scarf with pockets 66–69
  simple striped sweater 20–25
  toddler's socks 32–35
  toy basket 146–147
chunky cable lap blanket 130–131
chunky yarns 164, 165
circles cot blanket 26–29
circular knitting 224–226
  joining the circle of stitches 224
  knitting a Mobius loop 225
  knitting tubes 224–226
  working with circular knitting
    needle 224
  working with double-pointed
    needles 226
circular needles 169, 170, 224
cm 195
color block sweater 44–47
color wheel 166

charted colorwork 214
  check slip-stitch patterns 221
  holding the yarns 215–216
  see also Fair Isle; intarsia
cones 162
cont 195
"Continental" style knitting 176–177
contrast-edge cast-on 183
crochet cast-off 188

D
darning needle 170
dec 195
dec 1 195
decreases 195, 204–207
  decrease cast-off 189
  double decreases 206
  fully fashioned shaping 211
  knit two together 204
  paired decreases 208, 211
  paired edge decreases 210
  purl two together 204
  slip one, knit one, pass slipped
    stitch over 205
  slip, slip, knit 205
  slip, slip, purl 207
delayed cast-off 188
double cast-on 182
double decreases 206
double knit (DK) yarns 164, 165
double slipped garter selvage 231
double-pointed needles 169, 170,
  224, 226
double-twist-loop cast-on 181
dropped stitches, picking up 227
duplicate stitch 247
dye-lots 163

E
ear warmer headband 76–77
edge-to-edge seam 240
embellishments 244–247
  fringes 246
  pom-poms 244
  tassels 245

  see also embroidery stitches
embroidery stitches
  bullion stitch 247
  duplicate stitch 247
  lazy daisy stitch 247
  running stitch 246
"English" style knitting 175
equipment 154–171
  needles 168–169
  yarns 154–167
eyelash yarns 157
eyelets 232, 234

F
fabric yarns 161
Fair Isle
  baby Fair Isle cardigan 14–19
  charts 214
  easy Fair Isle sweater 82–85
  Fair Isle Christmas baubles 148–151
  Fair Isle coasters 142–143
  Fair Isle sweater dress 48–51
  garter stitch 218
  knit and purl 218
  knit weave 219
  Norwegian sweater 40–43
  partial Fair Isle sweater 90–95
  snowflake pillow 138–141
  stranding technique 215
  tea-cozy stitch 219
  two strand laying-in 219
  weaving in Fair Isle floats 216–219
fastenings 242–243
  snaps 242
  zips, sewing in 243
fibers 154
  see also yarns
fine yarns 164, 165
finger loop cast-on 180
finishing 228–243
  blocking 238
  eyelets and buttonholes 232–237
  fastenings 242–243
  picking up stitches 228–229
  picot hem 241

seams 239–241
selvages 230–231
  see also embellishments
5-6 ply yarns 164, 165
floats (Fair Isle), weaving in 216–219
foll 195
4-ply yarns 164, 165
14-ply yarns 164, 165
fringes 246
fully fashioned shaping 211

G
g 195
g st 195
garter selvages 230
garter stitch 192, 195
  baby booties 30–31
  child's beanie hat 54–55
  child's cowl hood 60–61
  child's striped scarf 56–59
  chunky cable lap blanket 130–131
  circles cot blanket 26–29
  Fair Isle 218
  patchwork blanket 132–137
  toy basket 146–147
gauge 163, 164, 195
gauge swatches 196
gauges, needle 170
grafted seam 240

H
hanks 162
hats
  baby pom-pom hat 12–13
  beanie hat 122–123
  cabled bobble hat 96–97
  child's beanie hat 54–55
  child's cowl hood 60–61
  child's hat with ear flaps 62–63
  men's slouchy hat 126–127
  simple baby beanie hat 10–11
  slouchy hat 98–99
holding yarn and needles 175–176
  colorwork 215–216
  "Continental" style 176

"English" style 175
holes, preventing 222-223
home
    cabled pillow cover 144-145
    chunky cable lap blanket 130-131
    Fair Isle Christmas baubles 148-151
    Fair Isle coasters 142-143
    patchwork blanket 132-137
    snowflake pillow 138-141
    toy basket 146-147
hooded scarf 70-73

I
in 195
inc 195
inc 1 195
increases 195, 198-203
    knit into front and back of
    stitch 198
    lifted increase on knit row 199
    "make-one" increase on a purl row 201
    "make-one" left cross increase on a
        knit row 199
    "make-one" right cross increase on
    a knit row 200
    multiple increases 201
    paired increases 208, 209, 211
    purl into front and back of stitch 199
    yarn-over at the beginning of a row
        203
    yarn-over between knit and purl
    stitches 203
    yarn-over between knit stitches 202
    yarn-over between purl stitches 202
intarsia 220
    charts 214
    circles cot blanket 26-29
    color changes 220
    sheep scarf with pockets 66-69
    two-color cables 220
invisible cast-on 185

J
jelly yarn 161
joining yarn 185

jumbo needles 168

K
k 195
k1 tbl 195
k2tog 195
kfb 195
knit stitch 190
    "Continental" style 176
    knit into front and back of
        stitch 198
    knit two together 204
    knit-on cast-on 179
    knit-stitch cast-on 179
    knitting through back of loop 197
    unpicking a knit row 227
knitting bags 171
knitting in the round see circular knitting
knitting needles see needles
knitting patterns see patterns
knitwise 195
knitwise, cast-off 186
knitwise, slipping stitches 197

L
labels, yarn 163
lace yarns 164, 165
laundry care 163
lazy daisy stitch 247
LH 195
lifted increase on knit row 199
long-tail cast-on 182
loop, knitting through the back of 197
loose-spun yarns 159

M
m 195
M1 195
M1k 195
"make-one" increases 199-201
    on a knit row 199-200
    on a purl row 201
mattress stitch 239
men's patterns
    beanie hat 122-123

cabled scarf 124-125
    men's slouchy hat 126-127
    ribbed socks 118-119
    textured sweater 114-117
mercerized cotton yarns 155
merino wool yarns 154
mistakes
    picking up a dropped stitch 227
    unpicking a knit row 227
    unpicking a purl row 227
mittens
    baby mittens 36-37
    child's easy mittens 74-75
mm 195

N
needle gauges 170
needle organizers 171
needles 168-169
    bamboo 168
    cable 168
    circular 169, 170
    conversion chart 169
    darning needle 170
    double-pointed 169, 170
    jumbo 168
    plastic 168
    point protectors 171
    straight 168
needles, holding
    "Continental" style 176
    "English" style 175
Norwegian sweater 40-43

O
oz 195

P
p 195
p2tog 195
paired decreases 208, 210
    paired edge decreases 210
paired increases 208, 209
    paired lifted edge increase 209
partial Fair Isle sweater 90-95

patt 195
patterns
abbreviations 195
altering 233
beginners 194
charts 194
following 194–196
stitch symbols 194, 195
terminology 195
written instructions 194, 196
pfb 195
pick up and knit 195
picking up stitches 228–229
along a curved edge 229
along row-ends 228
cast-on/off edge 228
dropped stitches 227
with a crochet hook 228
picot hem 241
picot loop selvage 231
pillows
cabled pillow cover 144–145
snowflake pillow 138–141
pins 170
plastic needles 168
plastic yarns 160
plied yarns 156
plies 164
point protectors 171
pom-poms 244
psso 195
purl stitch 191
"Continental" style 177
purl cast-off 187
purl into front and back of stitch 199
purl two together 204
unpicking a purl row 227
untwisting an incorrect stitch 177
purlwise 195
purlwise, slipping stitches 197

R
rem 195
rep 195
rev st st 195

reverse stockinette stitch 193, 195
RH 195
ribbing
casting off in rib effect 187
color block sweater 44–47
men's slouchy hat 126–127
Norwegian sweater 40–43
ribbed socks 118–119
toddler's socks 32–35
ribbon yarns 158
round, knitting in the see circular knitting
row counters 171
RS 195
rubber yarn 161
ruched scarf 104–105
running stitch 246

S
s 195
s1 k1 psso 195
s1 k2tog psso 195
s2 k1 p2sso 195
scarves
cabled scarf 124–125
child's striped scarf 56–59
hooded scarf 70–73
ruched scarf 104–105
sheep scarf with pockets 66–69
scissors 170
seams 239–241
backstitch seam 241
edge-to-edge seam 240
figure-eight start for seams 239
grafted seam 240
mattress stitch 239
three-needle cast-off 189
whipped stitch seam 240
selvages 230–231
chain selvage 231
double slipped garter selvage 231
garter selvage 230
picot loop selvage 231
slipped garter selvage 230
shaping
fully fashioned shaping 211

short row shaping 223
see also decreases; increases
sheep scarf with pockets 66–69
short cabled socks 106–109
short rowing 222–223
holes, preventing 222–223
short row shaping 223
silk yarns 155
simple baby beanie hat 10–11
simple striped sweater 20–25
single cast-on 178
single ribbing 193
16-ply yarns 164, 165
sk2p 195
skeins 162
skp 195
slipknot 174–175
slip one, knit one, pass slipped
stitch over 205
slip, slip, knit 205
slip, slip, purl 207
slipped garter selvage 230
slipping stitches
knitwise 197
purlwise 197
slubby yarns 157
snaps 242
snowflake pillow 138–141
socks
ribbed socks 118–119
short cabled socks 106–109
toddler's socks 32–35
sport yarns 164
ssk 195
st st 195
steam blocking 238
stitch holders 170
slipping stitches off the needle 186
stitch markers 171
stitch symbols 194, 195
charts 194
stitches
garter stitch 192
knit stitch 190
mattress stitch 239

picking up 228–229
purl stitch 191
reverse stockinette stitch 193
single ribbing 193
stockinette stitch 192
tea-cozy stitch 219
see also embroidery stitches
stockinette stitch
stockinette stitch 192, 195
child's beanie hat 54–55
ribbed socks 118–119
simple baby beanie hat 10–11
simple striped sweater 20–25
straight needles 168
stranding technique, Fair Isle 215
string yarn 161
stripes
child's striped scarf 56–59
simple striped sweater 20–25
st(s) 195
superfine yarns 164, 165
suspended cast-off 188
sweaters and cardigans
baby Fair Isle cardigan 14–19
cable and bobble sweater 86–89
color block sweater 44–47
easy Fair Isle sweater 82–85
Fair Isle sweater dress 48–51
Norwegian sweater 40–43
partial Fair Isle sweater 90–95
simple striped sweater 20–25
textured sweater 114–117
symbols, yarn labels 163
synthetic fibers 154, 155, 156, 158, 160

T
tape measures 171
tape yarns 158
tassels 245
tbl 195
tea-cozy stitch 219
textured sweater 114–117
thicknesses, yarn 164–165
three-needle cast-off 189
3-ply yarns 164, 165

thumb cast-on 178
toddler's socks 32–35
tog 195
tools see equipment
toy basket 146–147
tubular cast-on 185
tweed yarns 158
12-ply yarns 164, 165
twisted double cast-on 184
twists 212
2-ply yarns 164, 165

U, V
unpicking
knit row 227
purl row 227
visible increases see yarn-over increases

W
weights, yarn 164–165
wet blocking 238
whipstitch seam 240
wire yarn 160
women's patterns
boot cuffs 110–111
cable and bobble sweater 86–89
cabled bobble hat 96–97
easy Fair Isle sweater 82–85
partial Fair Isle sweater 90–95
ruched scarf 104–105
short cabled socks 106–109
slouchy hat 98–99
wrist warmers 100–101
wool yarns 154
work even 195
worsted yarns 164, 165
wrist warmers 100–101
WS 195

Y
yarn, holding
colorwork 215–216
"Continental" style 176
"English" style 175
yarn tail, winding up 178

yarn-over increases 195
yarn-over at the beginning of a row 203
yarn-over between knit and purl
stitches 203
yarn-over between knit stitches 202
yarn-over between purl stitches 202
yarns 154–167
acrylic 155
bouclé yarn 159
braided yarn 157
buying 162
chenille 156
colors 166–167
dye lots 163
eyelash yarn 157
fabric 161
fibers 154
jelly yarn 161
labels 163
loose-spun yarn 159
mercerized cotton 155
merino wool 154
natural and synthetic mixes 155
plastic 160
plied 156
ribbon yarn 158
rubber 161
silk 155
slubby yarn 157
string 161
synthetic fibers 154, 155, 156,
158, 160
tape yarn 158
tweed yarn 158
weights and thicknesses 164–165
wire 160
wool 154
yd 195
yo 195

Z
zippers, sewing in 243

Acknowledgments

Dorling Kindersley would like to thank the following people for their hard work and contributions toward *Winter Knits Made Easy*.

Knitting consultant Dr. Vikki Haffenden

Knitting designers Caroline Birkett, Sian Brown, Ruth Cross, Lara Evans, Margo Ewart, Julie Ferguson, Vikki Haffenden, Amanda Jones

Knitters Pauline Buck, Angela Corbett, Shirley Crawford, Christine Glasspool, Janet Morton

Pattern checker Carol Ibbetson

Proofreader Iona Bower

Indexer Marie Lorimer

Design assistance Vikas Sachdeva and Zaurin Thoidingjam

Initial planning and commissioning Katharine Goddard

Photography assistant Julie Stewart

Location for photography 1st Option and Light Locations

The following yarn manufacturers and distributors for supplying yarn for the projects Debbie Bliss, Coats Crafts UK, King Cole Ltd., Mirasol, Rico, and Sirdar Yarns

Models Amelia Amos, Alexander Cannell, Eva and Grace Lam, Niamh Long, Aiden Ng, India Odedra, Cavarni Pantelli, Kaylan Patel, Violet Peto, Edward Phillips, Ellie de Rose, Leo Rodway, Chris Stanton, and Abbie Tarrant

About the consultant

Dr. Vikki Haffenden has an active career encompassing all aspects of hand and machine knitting and knitwear design. She is the co-author of Dorling Kindersley's *The Knitting Book* and *Knit Step-by-Step* and the consultant on the *Big Book of Knitting* and *Baby and Toddler Knits Made Easy*. Her particular interest and expertise is the exploration and application of technical knitting for the design development of knitted textiles and garment shapes. Vikki holds a PhD based in commercial knitting and knitwear design research, and currently teaches in the department of Fashion Textiles at the University of Brighton in Sussex.

Happy knitting